From CHECKERED CLOTH

A Collection of Poetry 1990 Through the Present

ALLEN FRANK MCNAIR

Library of Congress Control Number: 2021900962

HARDBACK: 978-1-954673-93-9
PAPERBACK: 978-1-954673-92-2
EBOOK: 978-1-954673-94-6

Ordering Information:

For orders and inquiries, please contact:
1-888-404-1388
www.goldtouchpress.com
book.orders@goldtouchpress.com

Printed in the United States of America

Contents

Illustrations

Dedication

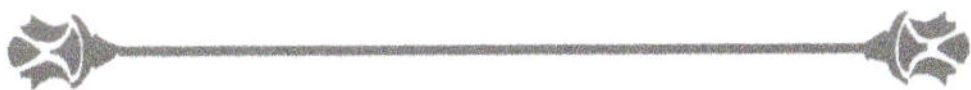

*This current edition of my poetry is dedicated to my wise friend, Darius Loghmanee,
who has supported me and offered sage counsel during the many years of our association*

Acknowledgements

This current anthology is the product of my years of my extensive experience with the written word. The original anthology contained the black and white illustrations included in this book. The writings in that book evolved from my brief time as a homeless person after my graduation from Columbia College Chicago. This book is an extension of my experience with the counseling services of the Thresholds Dincin Center and with the Bezazian Writers Group, a group originally formed as part of the now-defunct Neighborhood Writing Alliance.

As I have said before in my acknowledgements from my first published book, I Dream of A'maresh, I owe my immense gratitude for the encouragement and tough love shown by my parents, Wilbur and Sylvia McNair, who encouraged my efforts to practice my craft of written communication in creative ways to a wide audience of readers.

Again, I would like to thank my sister, Patty McNair for her enormous support of my various forays into the mysterious realm of writing and her loving advice for my continued efforts in this chosen field.

--to Waseem Rahman who has always good-naturedly challenged me in my editing of his own written work as he has navigated the educational waters to endeavor to acquire a PhD in his chosen field of Art Theory;

--to my brother Paul McNair, who taught me to write a good story for wider audiences;

--to the helpful and courteous members of the Bezazian Writers Group, especially Jill A. Charles, who encouraged me to reach an international audience through her acceptance of my writing and illustrations for the Batayan magazine;

--to Andrea Catalina Vaca, of the Knack Magazine, who actively sought me out after hearing my poetry at the Weeds Open Mic at the Hideout and accepted the first chapter of my first book along with other samples of my writing for the #51 issue of her publication;

--to Brighid O'Shaughnessy, who encouraged me to always deepen my understanding of the writer's craft, especially with my first book;

--to Darius Loghmanee, for his encouragement that I consult my peers when making any major decision regarding my expression of my desires for success and recognition;

--to every person who ever showed a burning desire for the acquisition of good literature and actively pursued this laudable goal.

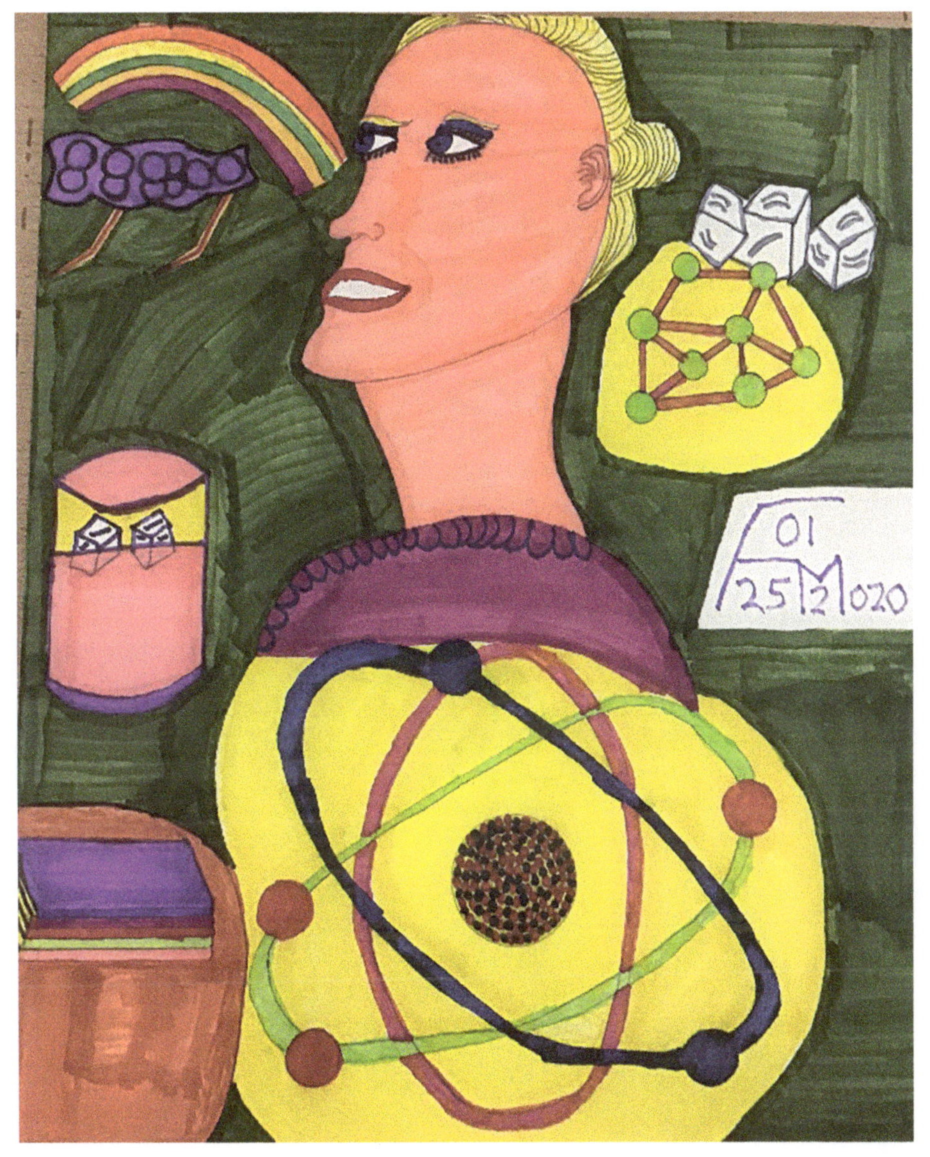

From Checkered Cloth Revisited
(2020-01-25)

From Checkered Cloth

Allen F. McNair©   June 19, 1991

The flower opens to greet
The sun's golden food as
It touches her delicate
Fingers of red.

The neighbors blush in
Pink hues, blossom in
Bold velvet blues, ignite
In yellow flames, shining.

From red checkered cloth a honey
Blonde head looks up, her blue
Eyes drink in these colors,
Cheek held against chilled glass.

She smiles and mimics a bunny's
Wriggling nose, her merry laugh
Jiggles pink lemonade and ice.
Her hand reaches back to find his.

She feels close to the view and him.
Sky and earth move
For her with their touch.
Her drink tastes as sweet as the day.

He watches the way she
Watches the scene.
His thoughts move in the lazy
Way the clouds wander by.

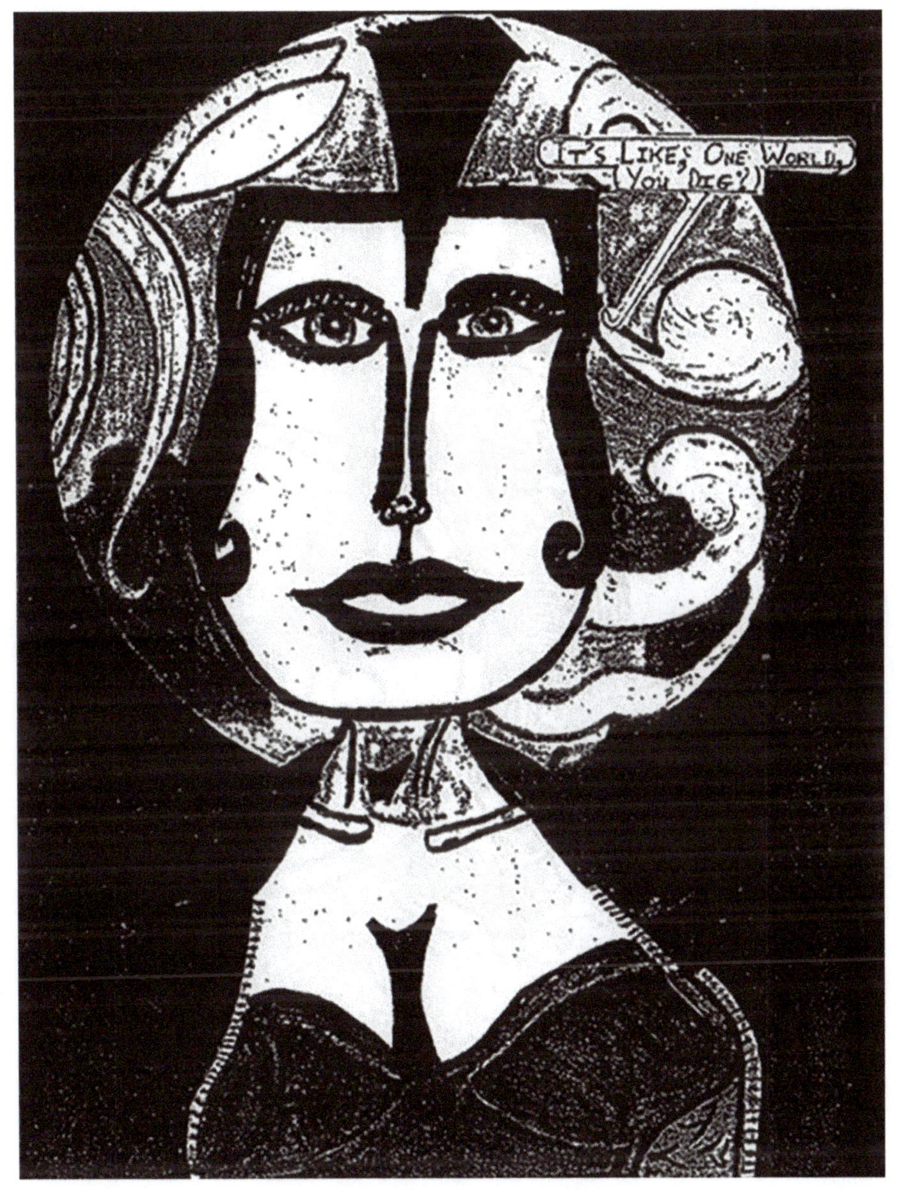

One World, You Dig?

From Checkered Cloth—Revisited

Allen F. McNair©   October 22, 2004

From the flower's golden petals
To the colorless sap within
A river almighty flows all through
Long stem and fluttering leaf.

The chilled glass of pink lemonade is
Only another form of this frozen bliss.
Held against a cheek whose cold
Red jewels rush life's fluid to the surface.

The atoms within her blood spin dizzily
With the close contact of icy glass
Against cooling skin so radiantly fresh.
Miniature planets revolve around tiny suns.

Two hands touching, lightly squeezed.
Galaxies of atoms race within each.
The rush to closeness without
Mirrors the flight of molecules within.

From red checkered cloth strong
Weaves of a special, sacred pattern.
Two bodies and souls entwined.
Love from its roots grows outwards.

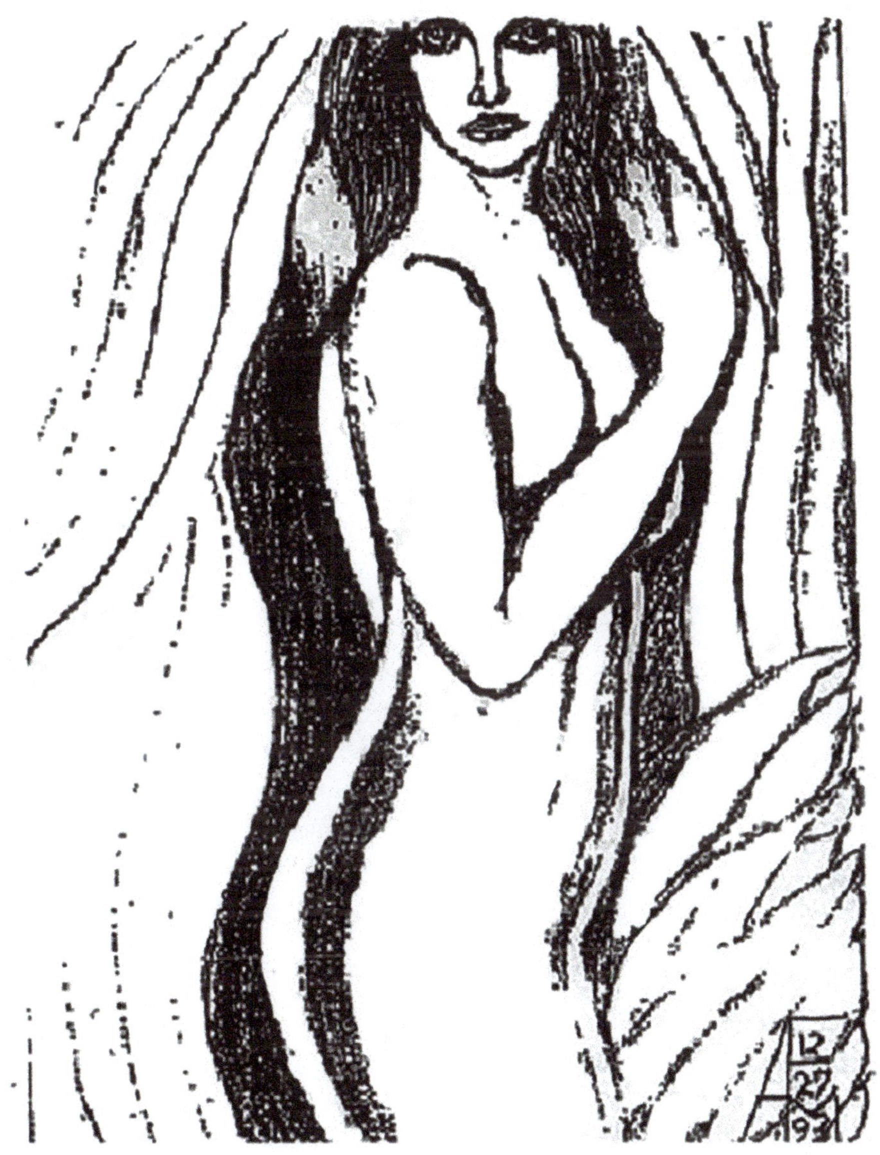

Face in the Candlelight

Sleeplessness

Lie in bed
Thoughts racing,
Regrets, missed chances,
Arguments made or unspoken.

Voices of friends,
Acquaintances, family, lovers,
Or those who refuse love
Screw the head on tighter.

Run away? No.
Blank my mind forever? No.
Go back to the day before?
Always no. Why not, yes?

Tension builds, must get up.
Body screams, needs to sleep.
Tension builds, body screams.
A furious war of mind and muscle.

Urge to strike someone,
Need to hurt oneself.
Strike! Hurt! Lash out!
Can only lash inside.

One hour in the bed
Then another, flies by.
Flopping under covers
Like some just-landed fish.

Maybe write another poem.
Possibly add to a story.
Fury can't stop the muse.
Sometimes spurs the creation.

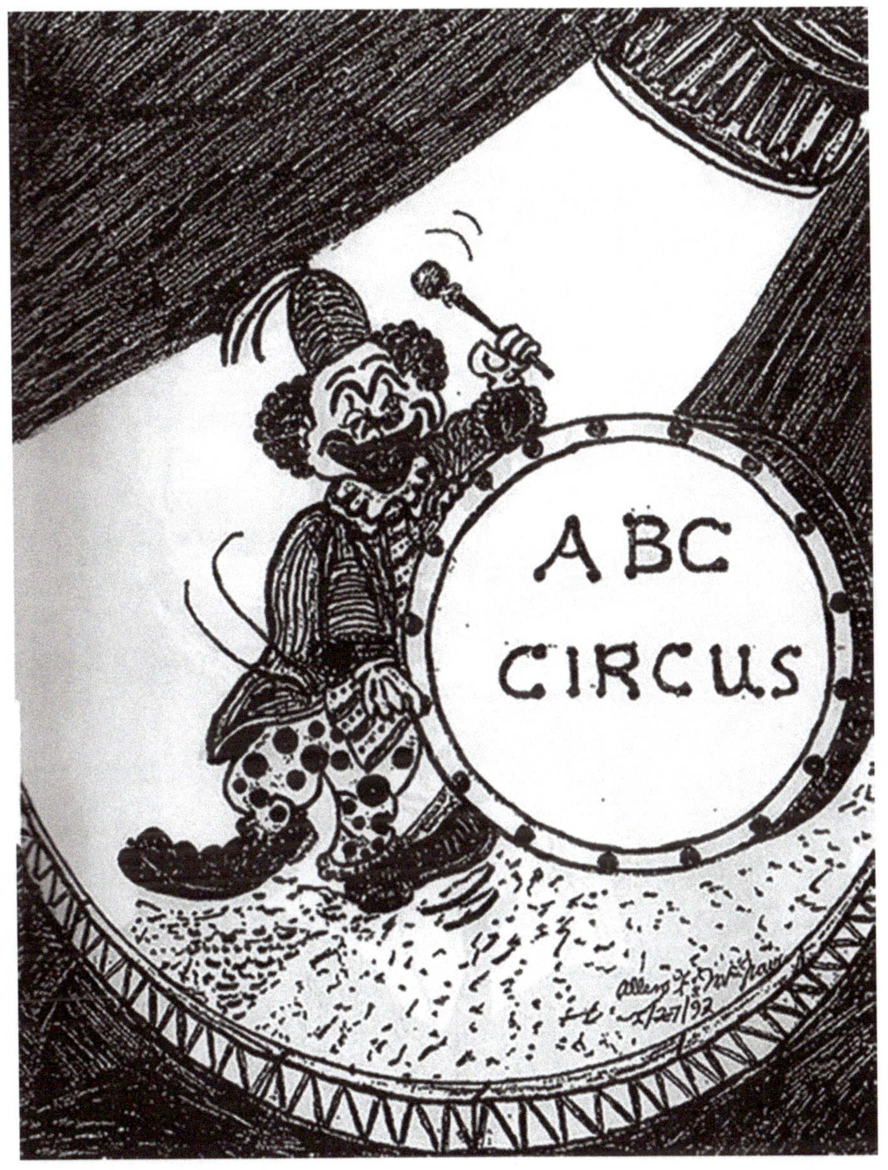

Circus Clown

Sleepy Day Start

Coffee in the morning,
Sleepy day start,
World a bright blur
Until I find my glasses.

A bear of a man
In boxer shorts,
Hairy chest a dark
Forest of hills and valleys.

His heavy feet
Tramp upstairs.
Wrought iron banister
Creaks beneath his hand.

His fear escapes from
Alcohol-haunted eyes.
"Wake up people!"
This god-man roars.

Does his family—
His wife, three sons,
His cutest little girl—
Exist before they stumble awake?

His craggy face, some
Wrinkled, old balloon,
Bobs, through crack of door.
His voice explodes quiet meditation.

Disturbing still transcendence,
He shakes my shoulder.
Percolations of confidence
Dissolve in wakefulness.

Crimson spider webs
Crisscross whites of his
Quick-shifting eyes.

Falling in the depths of mine, "You'd
Better get dressed for the trip downtown."
Coffee dribbles from chin that is
Doubled by life's own reality.

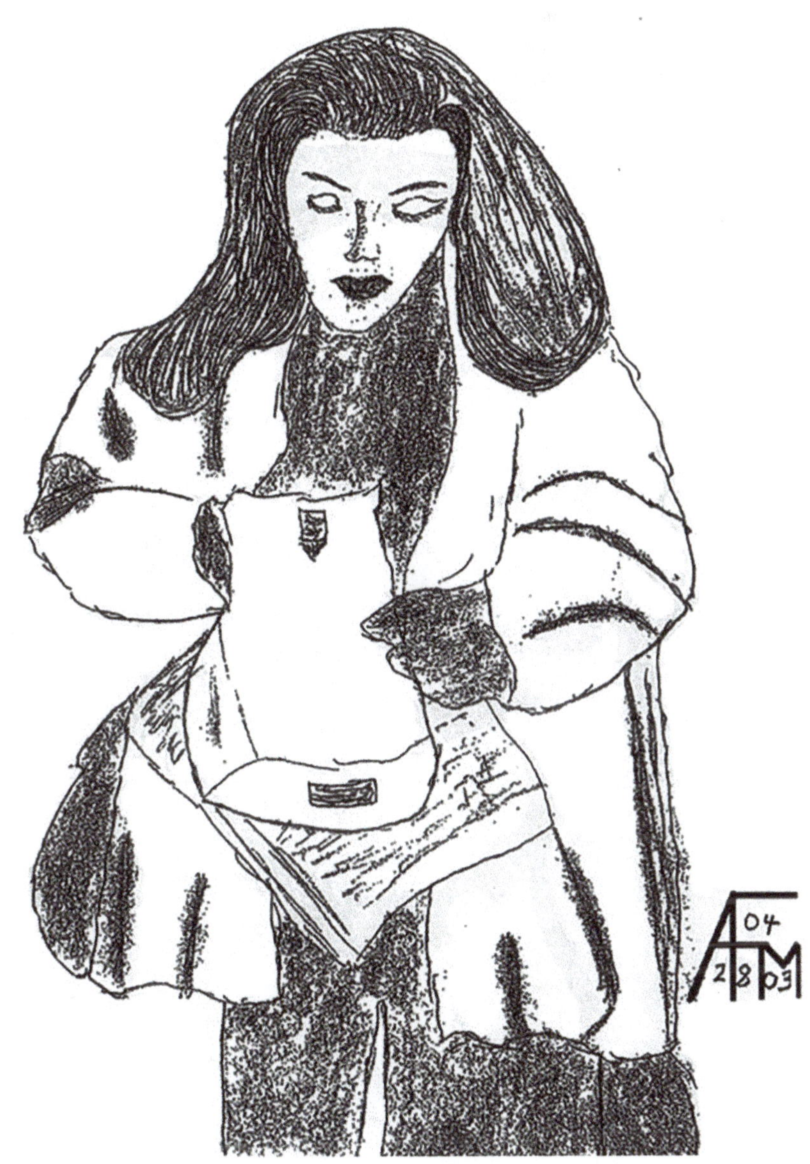

Dressed for Success

. . . In the Shadows

He'd seen her only once,
In a nameless hallway,
Under a poorly-lit arch.

He spied her from
A car window on his
Way to an art gala.

And her image, those
Wild features of her,
Like strong thought

Of love, survives.
As in that song,
"Photograph is framed…"

Her face, first a
Bubble of perception
And certain longing,

In the half-light, amid
The shadows and forms,
Amid the promises and mysteries.

Afraid this light
Ripple on his consciousness
Would burst in the froth

Of his exhibit, the
Noisy tedium of explanations
To careless viewers.

Something that came
From the flash and
The fire of pure intuition.

That part of her
Face in the shadows,
A mystery in mauve.

Shadows (continued)

The brightly lit part, like
The flare of a match just
Struck in the hard, raw florescence.

Fox collar of red
Cupped to her chin,
The color of cream, by a slim hand

As she turned
The shaded area of her face
Into the light.

Slim legs, color of smoke,
Moved further apart, to take
Firmer purchase of concrete beneath.

Hint of fire
Through a quick parting
Of her long fox coat.

* * * * *

You might forget where you saw her,
In some swank part of town
Where lofts have been transformed into
High-ceilinged chic apartments.
Or in those soft gray areas which still

Contain their wet, newspaper-strewn streets
And the empty warehouses that will never
Discover rehabilitation before being
Leveled into empty lots of gravel.

While you might forget
Just where you saw her,
You never forgot the
Slight curve of her smile.

Just imagine the pout that
Hides behind it, daring you to wipe
It away with presents and unending
Devotion to her every whim.

"I know you. Yes,
You in that passing car window."
Smiling curved lips, without
Forming the words, "I know

What you'd like. But I'm not
Really what you want. Only what
You choose to see in me
Is your true desire."

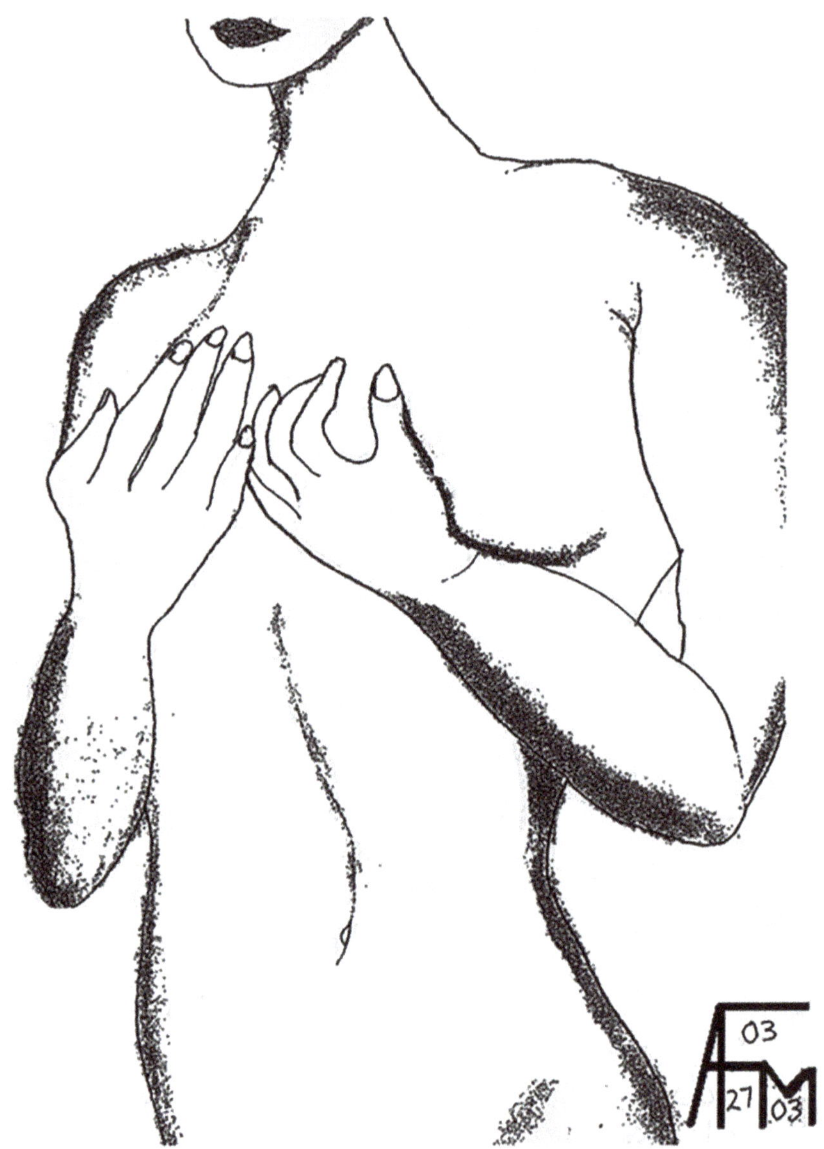

Faceless Nude

I Color in Moonlight

The colors of my crayons
Are different when I shade
In the moonlight of my bedroom.
They are tinged with silver.

The book I color in
Shows family life.
I see green as blue to
Shade the sky.

I see red as brown to
Paint the wooden fence.
All the crayons get mixed
Up, like our family often is.

The pale darkness hides
Wild thoughts of confusion.
Its blanket covers my strange
Fears of parents' loud rages.

I blindly sort my crayons
When unknown sound creaks.
The feelings are jumbled the
Same way the colors are at night.

Queen Bee

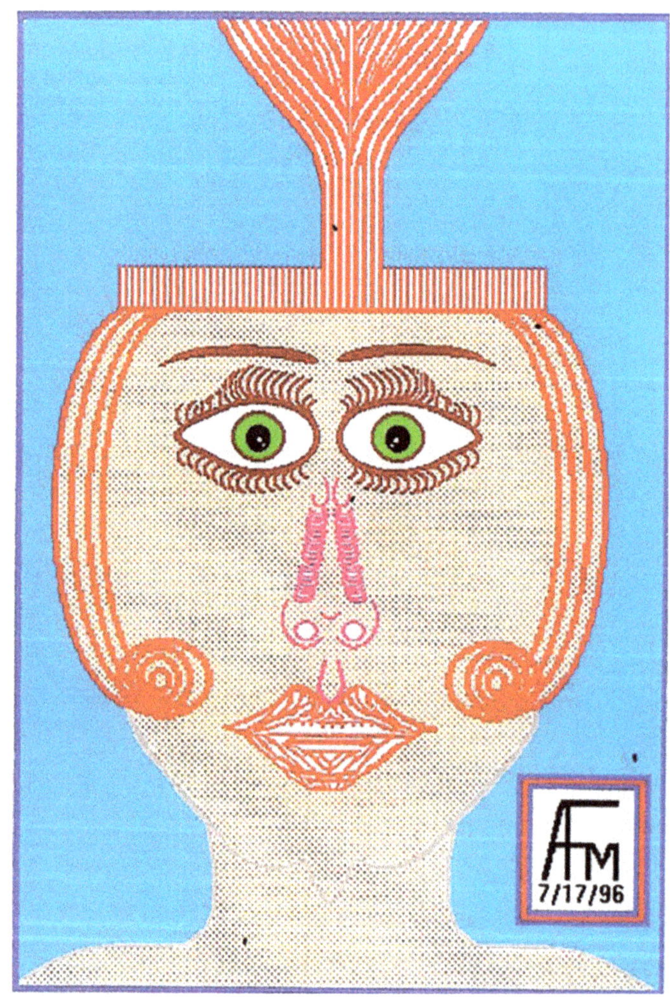

Telephone dangles by fragile
Metal cord under sole street
Lamp, a faint sound of ocean
From it, into no one's ear.

Night's neon lights up small
Donut shop where the black
And blue riders swarm around
Their red and brown queen bee.

Beneath her tough open leather
Jacket she flaunts her bustier
To match her crimson crest
Of sparse hair, high Mohawk.

Hypnotic eyes of sea green
Mask her vulnerability to
Life's transience—revolving
Door of friends and lovers.

Chalk cliffs of her face declare
Her mastery of the night, her
Fierce leadership of the street.
The boom box howls her disdain.

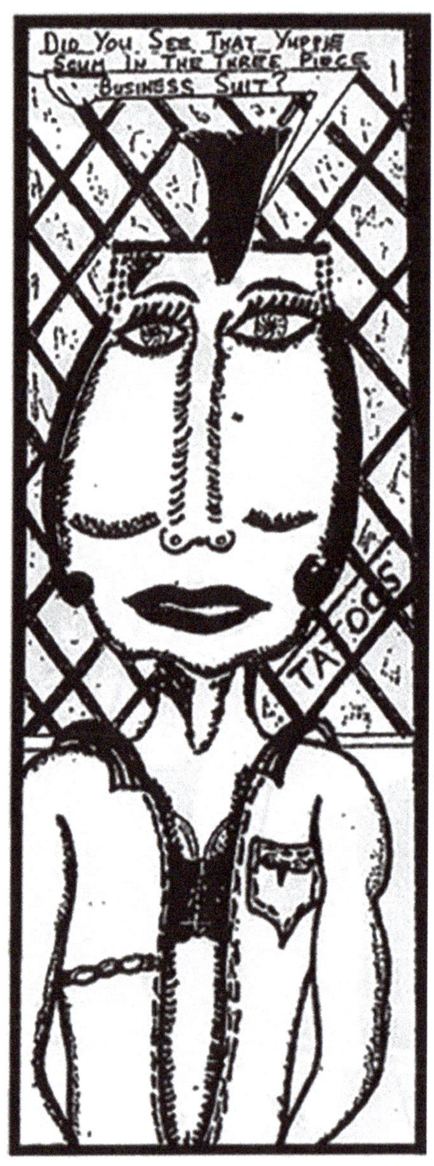

Queen Bee Comics, Panel 1

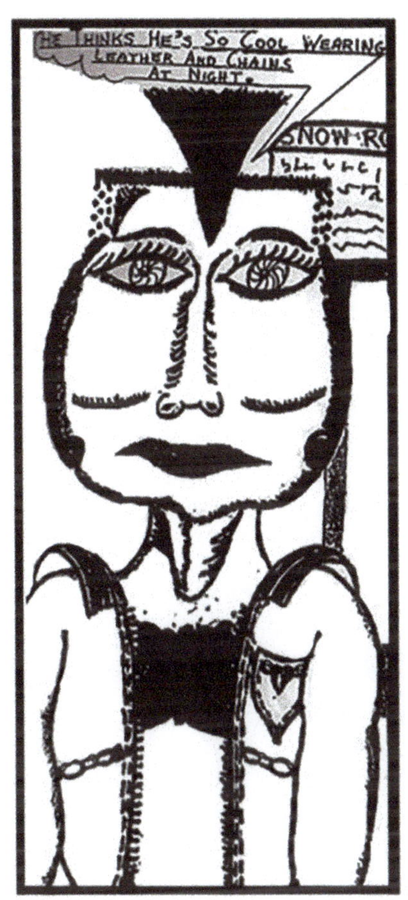

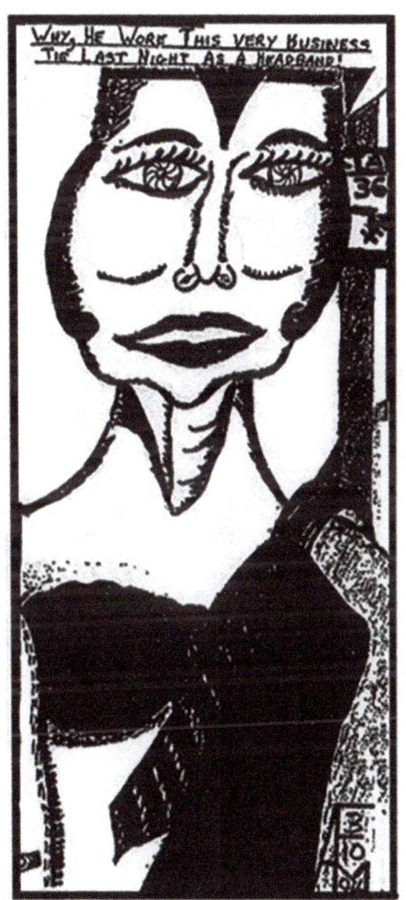

Queen Bee Comics, Panel 2

Comic Book Fever

I lie in bed, my throat dry and sore,
Fever places my head on fire.
Food tastes mostly of paste,
My head feels the rough texture
Of a sack of potatoes.

My nose is an emery board,
Unable to touch another tissue.
But mom has chicken soup,
It's taste not forgotten
By long-dead taste buds.

And now my spirit soars higher
Than my dizziness along with
Superman and Wonder Woman.
Their villains between the
Pages are mine as well.

My battle against cold's sinister enervation.
It is waged alongside Superman when he
Finds Kryptonite used against him by his
Current archenemy—Lex Luther,
Metallo, or the Fiendish alien, Brainiac.

I imagine the tenderness of the bold
Amazon if I were discovered on her
Secret island home and she nursed
Me back to virile health.

Or maybe Supergirl might wander
Into my home, suffering amnesia.
Receiving my help and nurture,
She might naturally love me in return.

Colds are often made so much
Lighter by super-heroes.

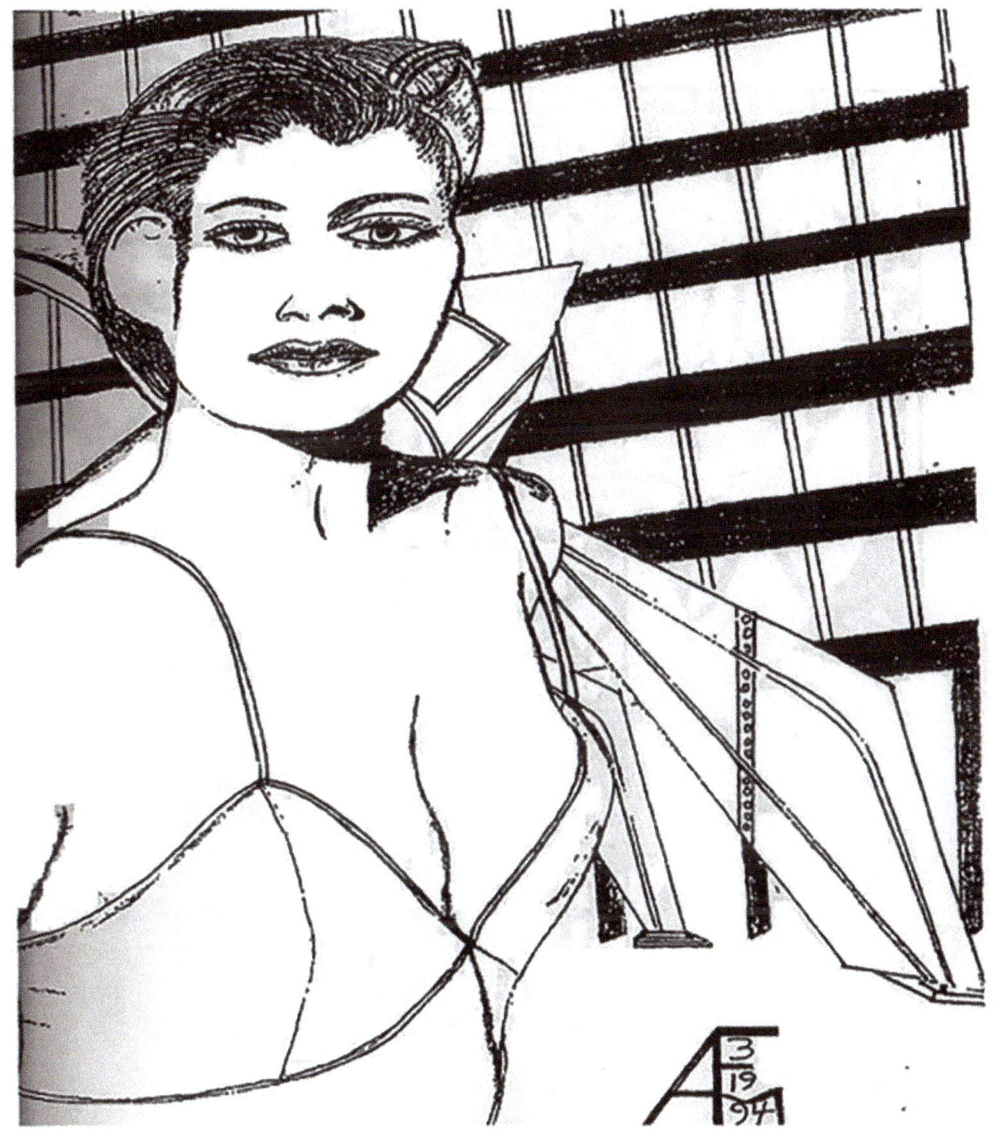

High-rise Beauty

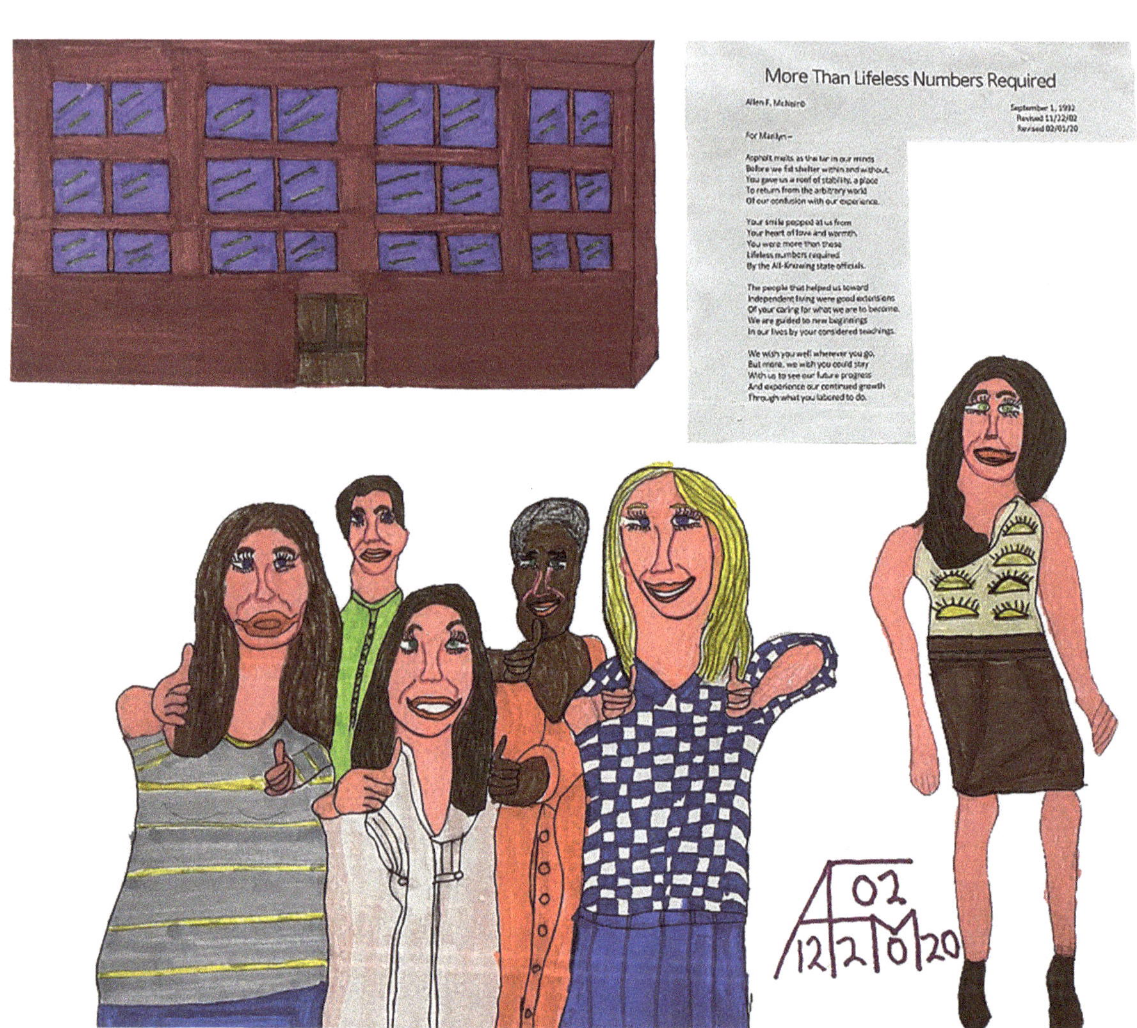

More Than Lifeless Numbers Required
(2020-02-21)

More Than Lifeless Numbers Required

(For Marilyn)

Asphalt melts as the tar in our minds
Before we find shelter within and without.
You gave us a roof of stability, a place
To return from the arbitrary world
Of our confusion with our experience

Your smile popped at us from
Your heart of love and warmth.
You were more than those
Lifeless numbers required
By the All-Knowing state officials.

The people that helped us towards
Independent living were good extensions
Of your caring for what we are to become.
We are guided to new beginnings
In our lives by your considered teachings.

We wish you well wherever you go.
But more, we wish you could stay
With us to see our future progress
And experience our continued growth
Through what you labored to do.

09/02/92
Revised 11/22/02
Revised 02/01/20

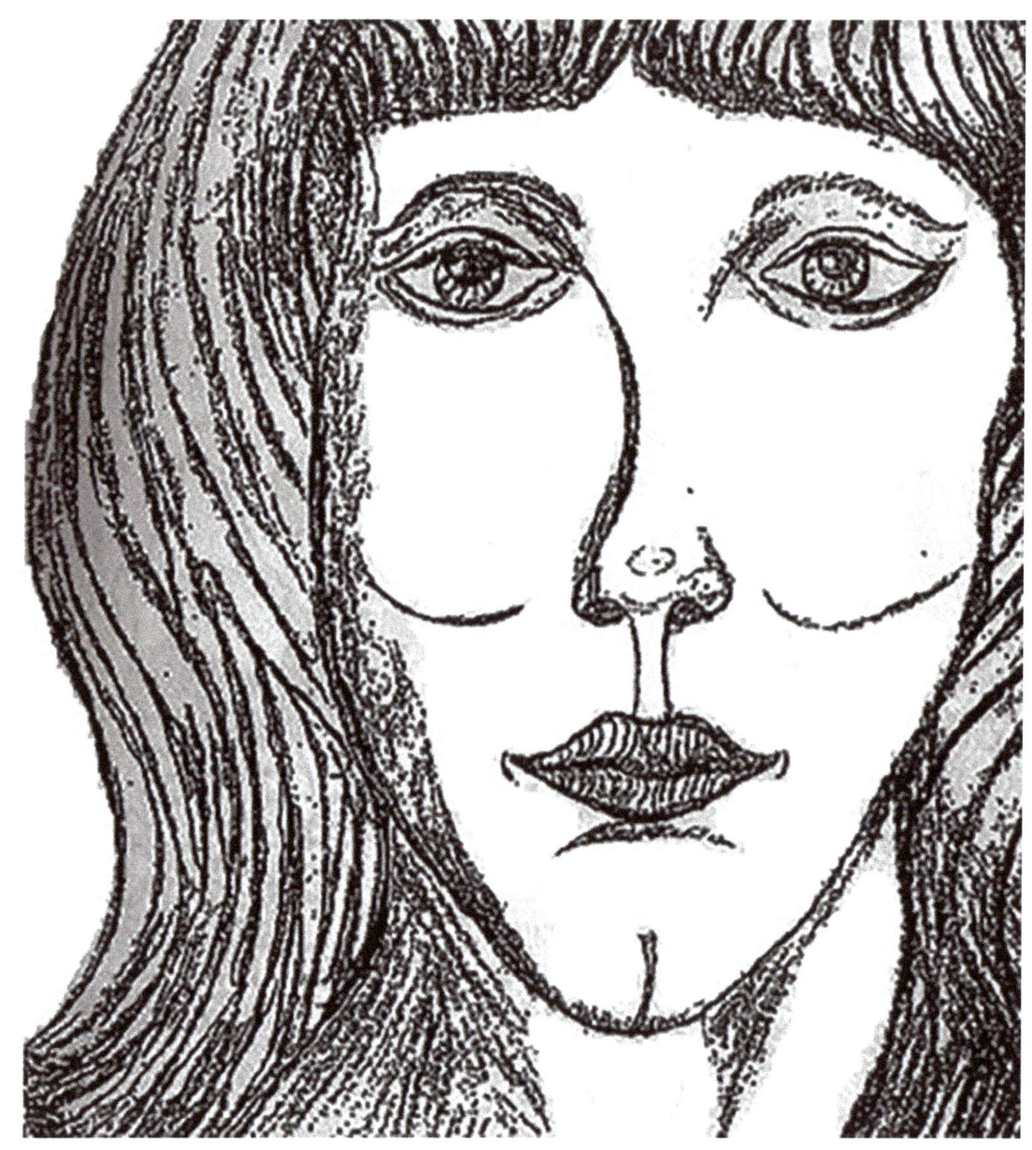

Rachel

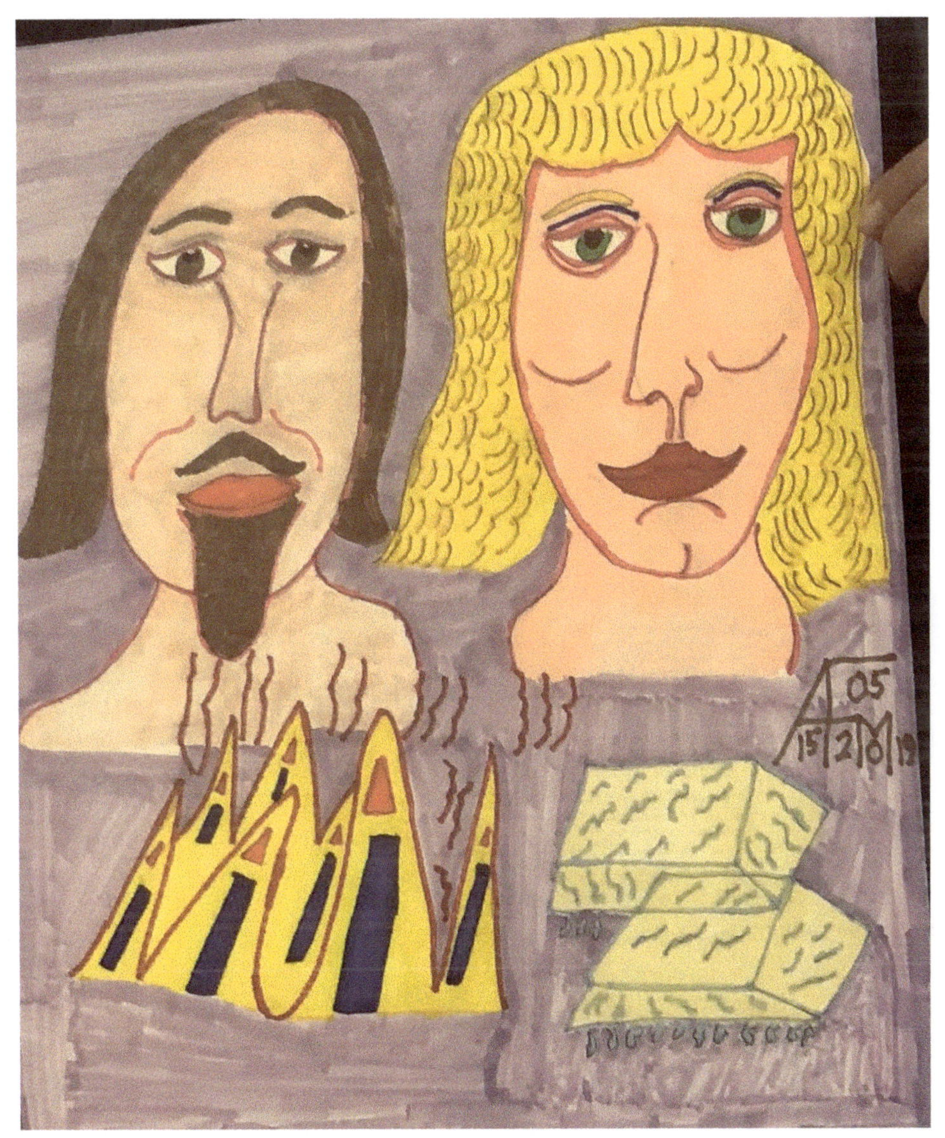

Fire and Ice
(2019-11-25)

Fire and Ice

Your fire and ice
Consumes my soul
And breaks my heart.
It shatters like brittle glass.

I burn for your passion,
A candle quickly burned up.
Your ideas, opinions fascinate.
Even when I don't agree.

You are cold to yourself,
Wanting to be elsewhere
And another person entire.
You deserve your own love.

You know the feelings of others,
Your heart warms to them.
Who is there to reach yours?
I am here to know who you are.

Winter comes but does not stay;
Frost is on the trees but awhile.
Let me be your spring today,
You will be my summer tomorrow.

We will see the grass green
Together. Ice will cool our drinks,
Not freeze our fresh friendship.
Blue will remain in the sky.

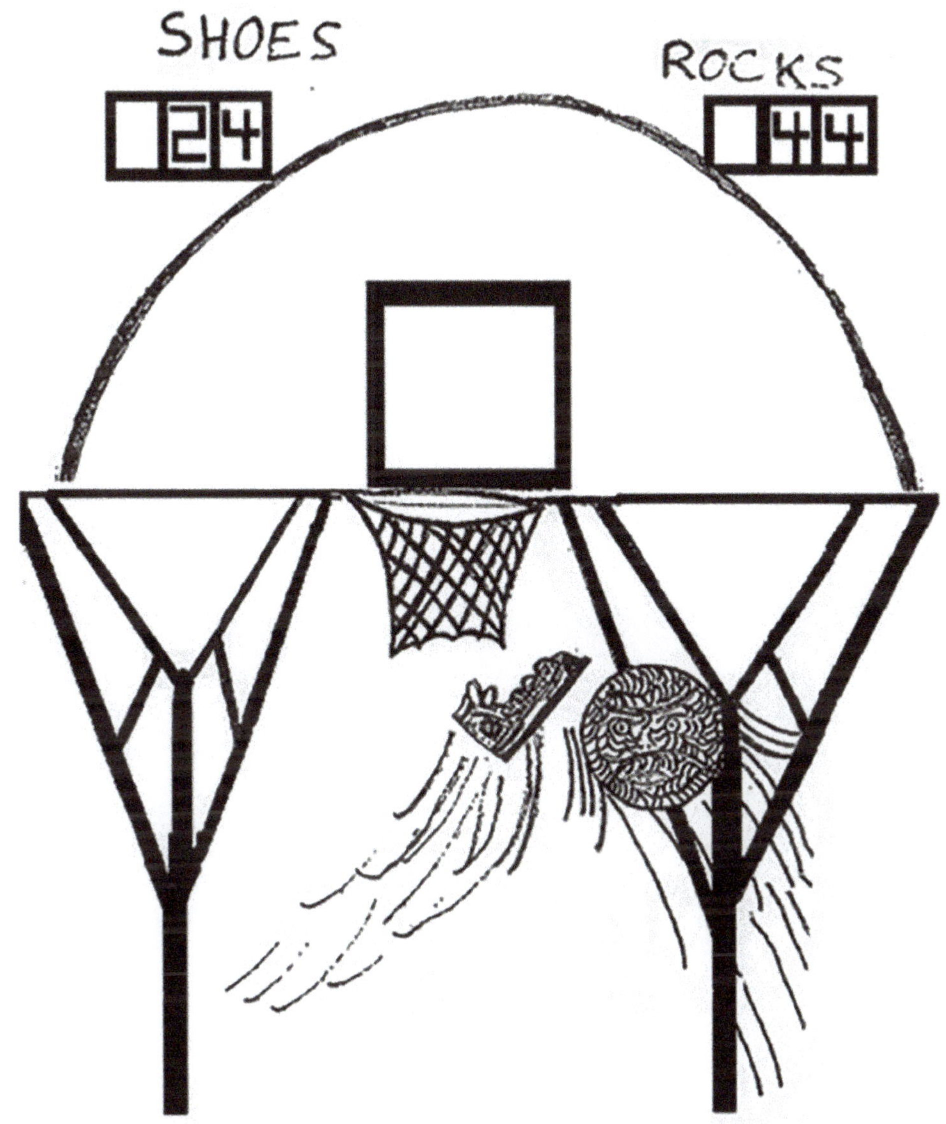

Shoes and Rocks Basketball

Scampering, Always Scampering

The rats are before the kitchen door.
Scampering, always scampering
To find good things to eat.

Chicken's blood to slake their thirst,
Scraps of liver give them the iron that
They crave for limbs so nimble for
Their fast scurrying escapes.

The cavalry charge of swift feline put them
All to rout, one hapless old one caught up in
Sharp claws of enemy merciless.

Toy before Meal, he is tossed and
Battered, tenderized while still alive.
His little nerves rattled, past victories
Shaken from his very muscles.

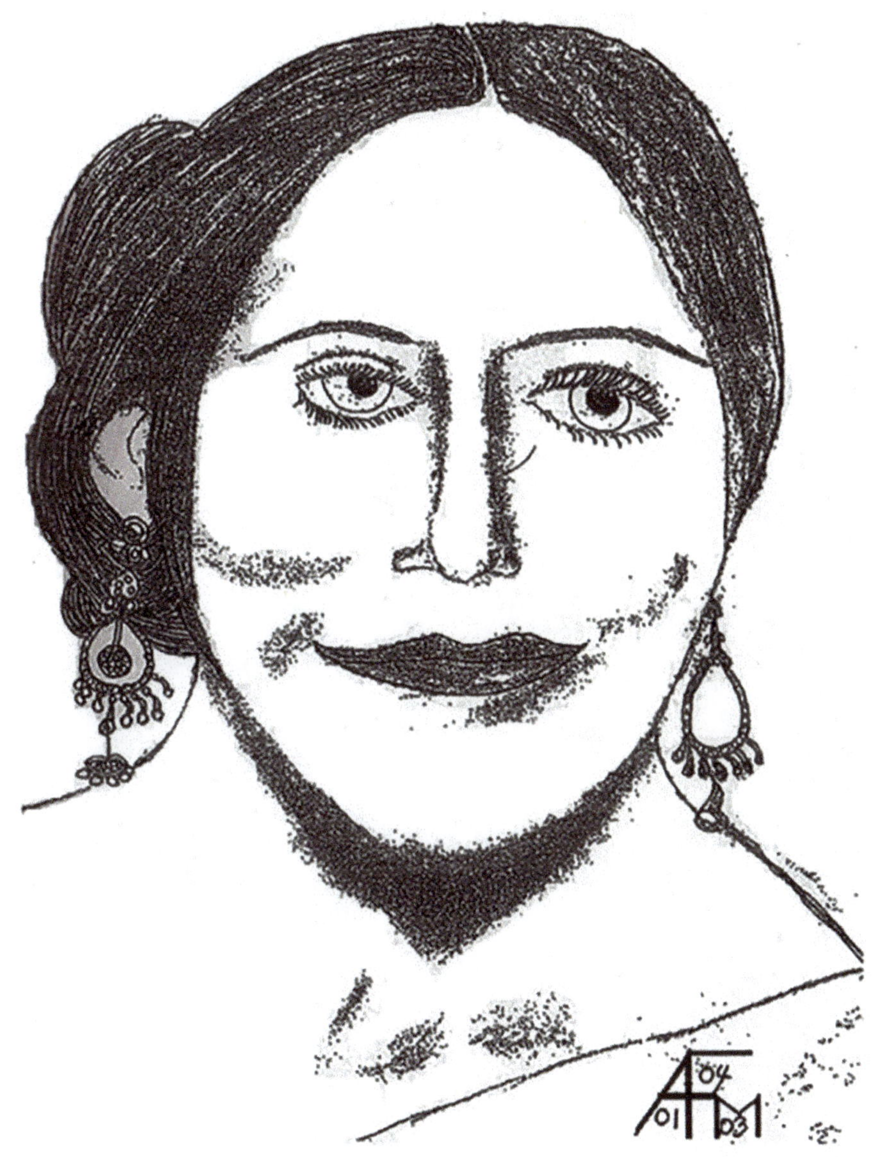

Spanish Rosita

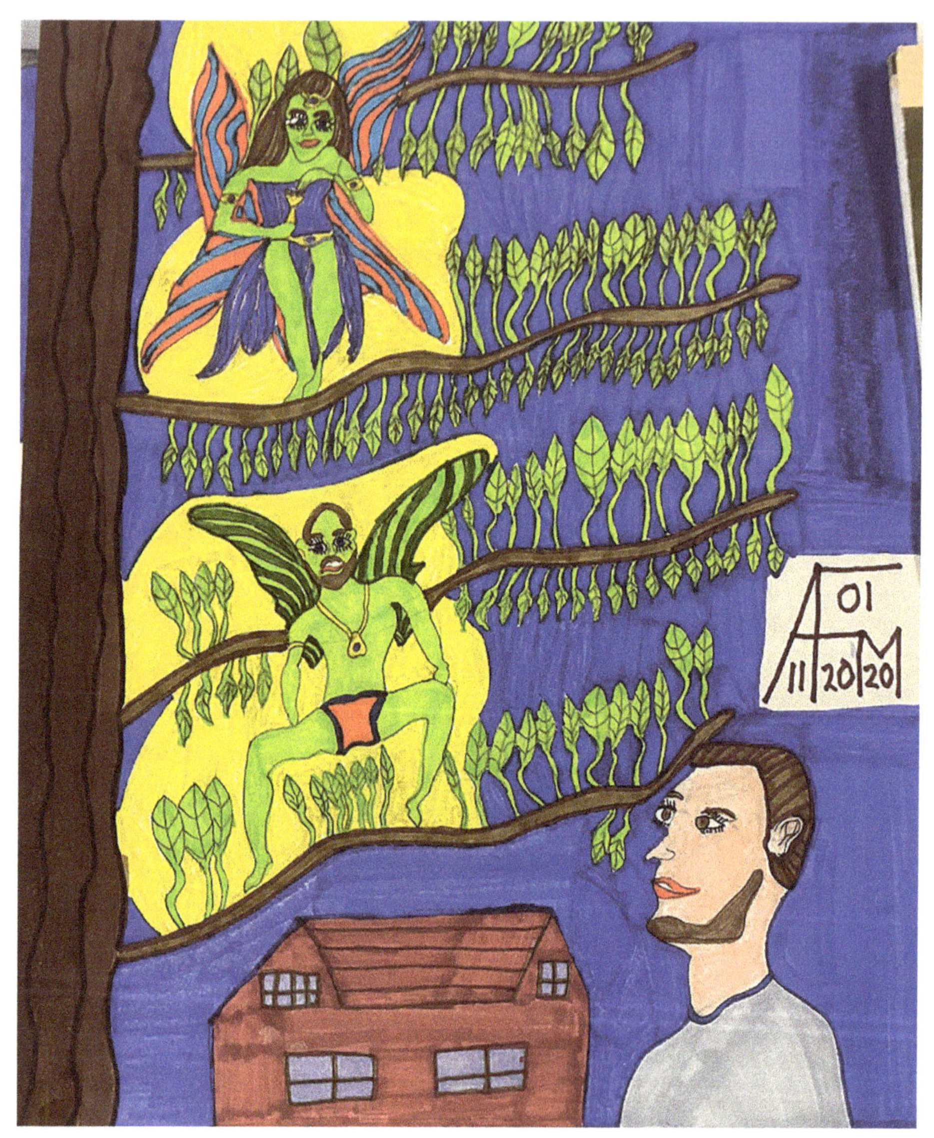

Slightest Bells Tinkling
(2020-01-17)

Slightest Bells Tinkling

By a ghostly light of a moon full.
I saw the sprightly dance of fairies.
The small sparks of magic circled
A thick, twisted tree all around.

The night air was so still & quiet, I
Heard the slightest bells tinkling.
In That moment in time, I stood frozen.
Sparkling white they were, pale colors.

Showered from waving hands miniature,
From dancing feet that dazzled in turns,
My own limbs lifted to follow their steps
And gestures in poor imitation.

Lemon drops, stardust filled my mind as I
Still watched what I could not believe.
Did I eat something to create this vision's beauty?
Creamed corn & beef seem too crude and course.

One face, only as large as my eye, stands out from
All the fairies—pearl white covered with spun gold.
Eyes of sapphire sweet lips of ruby,
She is somehow familiar to me.

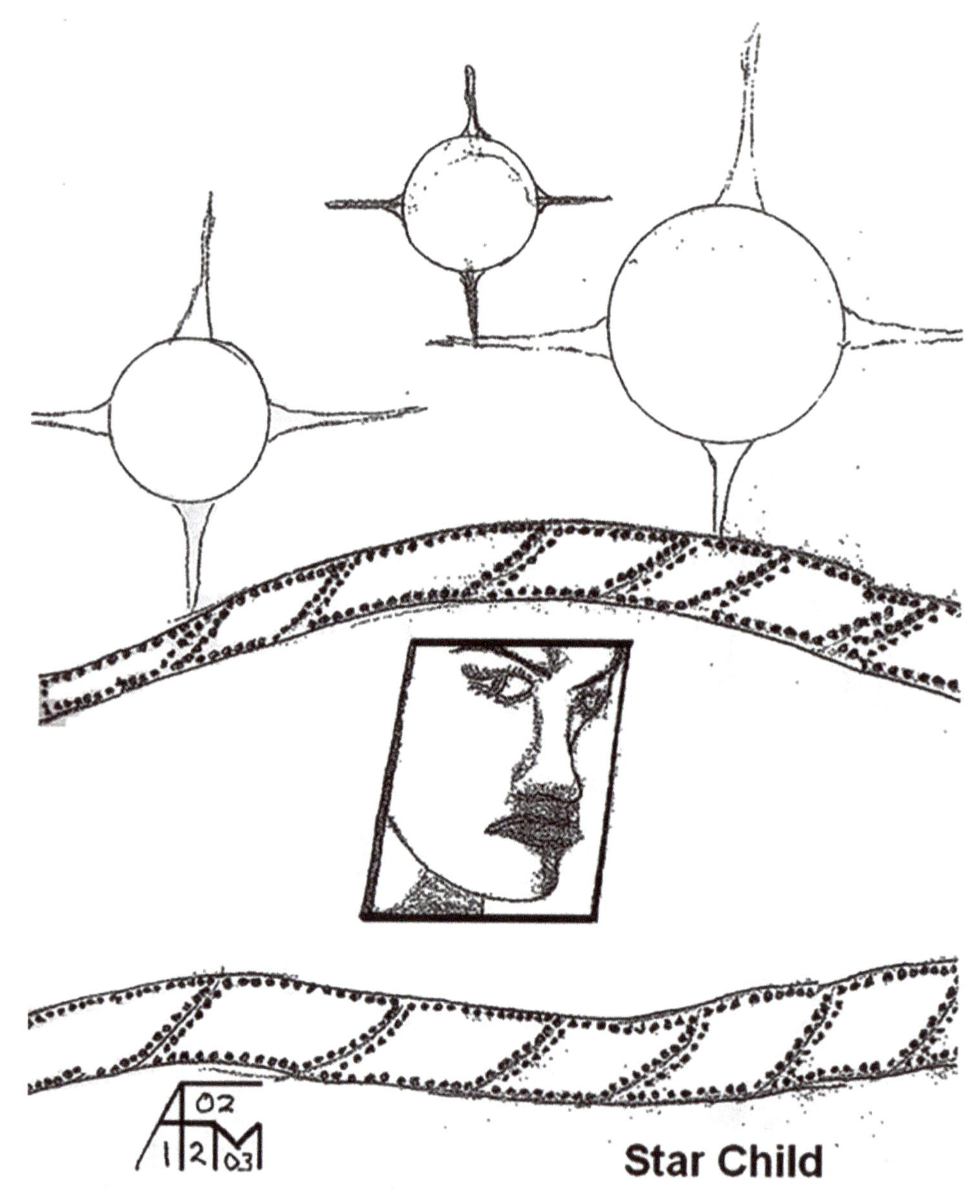

Star Child

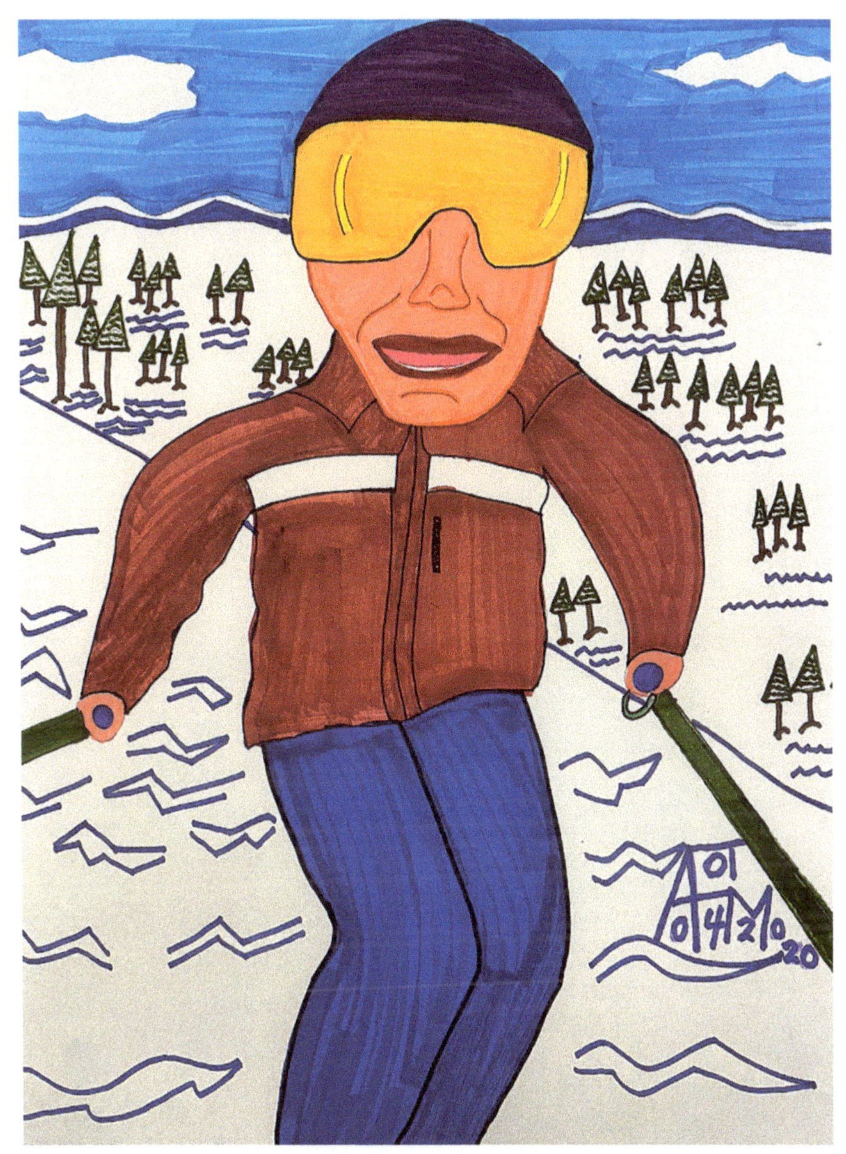

Before New Adventure
(2020-01-04)

Before New Adventure

For Mark—

His breath opens his lungs
To the sharp pain of ice and air.
His eyes travel to those

On different plains of
Snow, rock, and among
The frosted trees below.

For balance and motion,
Only two supple sticks.
His feet set upon two thin flatnesses

Under heavy boots. Poised
Before new adventure
On virgin ground, ready

To let gravity capture him,
To pull him forward.
He is the king of speed.

He pushes forward to
Leave his old world of
Frozen thoughts and ice.

1/31/93
Revised 11/22/02

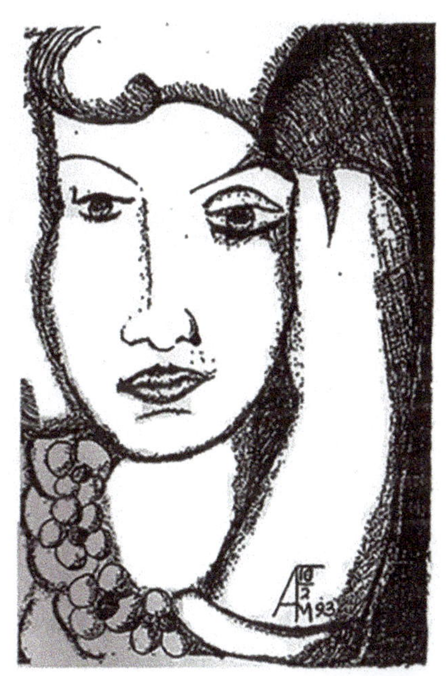

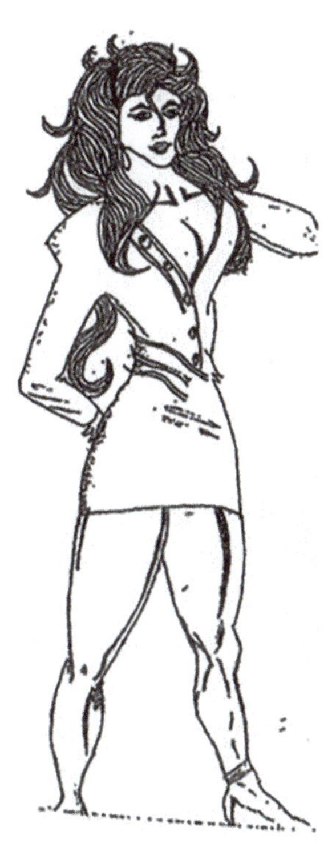

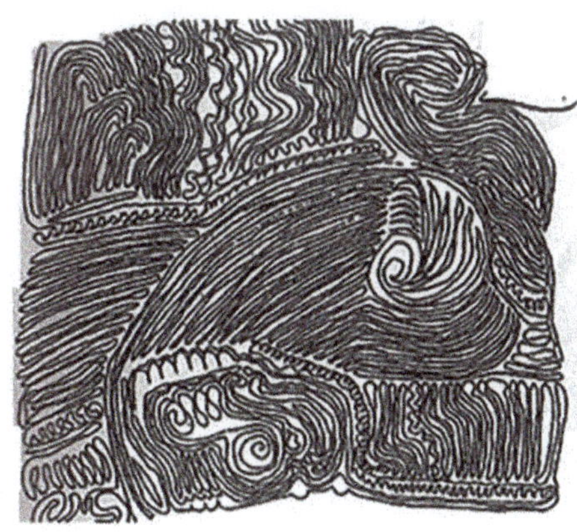

A Collection of My Art

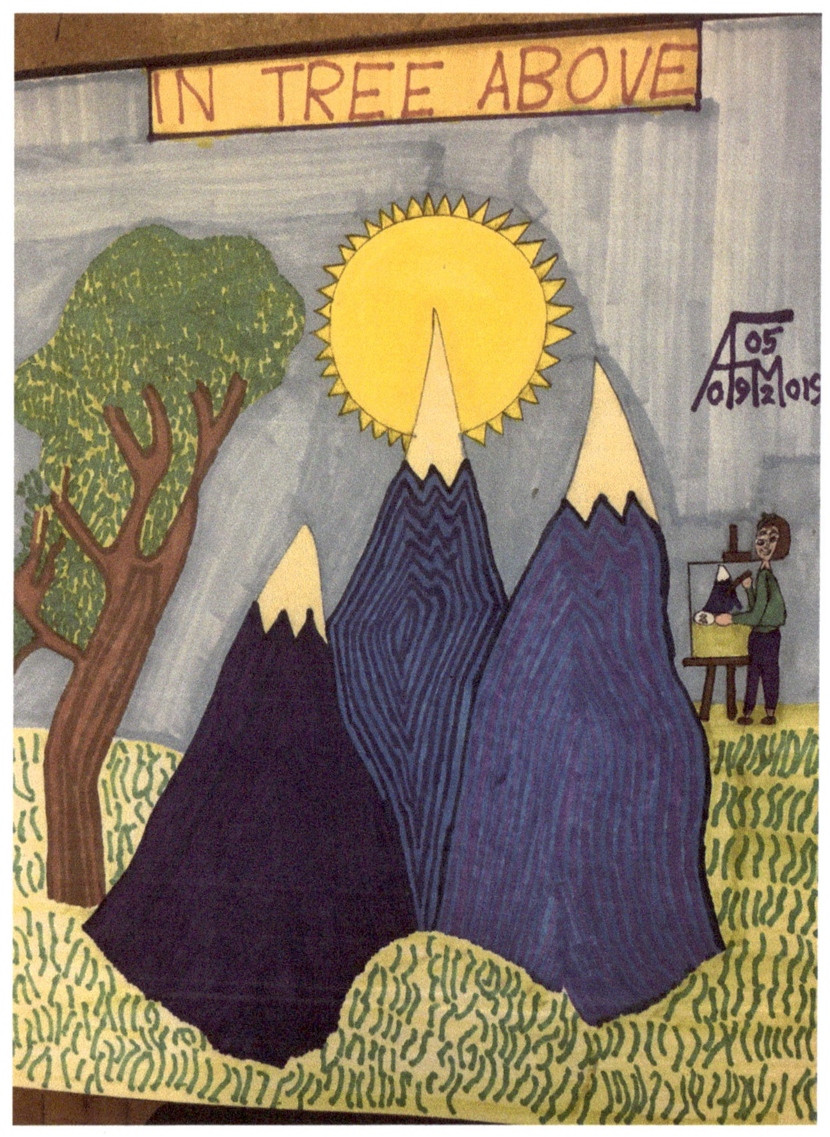

In Tree Above
(2019-09-05)

In Tree Above

For Heather—

Flowers purple feather
Her fresh face, the color
Of the sun's rays.

The lively bird sees specks
Race across wild grass
And stars of yellow that rise

Toward light blue vault.
Clouds wrap her face
With cool wetness,

Veil sharp eyes that flash at mice,
Snakes or the occasional person
Who throws herself to the ground

Covered by soft yellow spread.
Perched in a tree above the crowd
Of activity, she sits alone to view
The lesser world below.

1/31/93
Revised 11/22/02

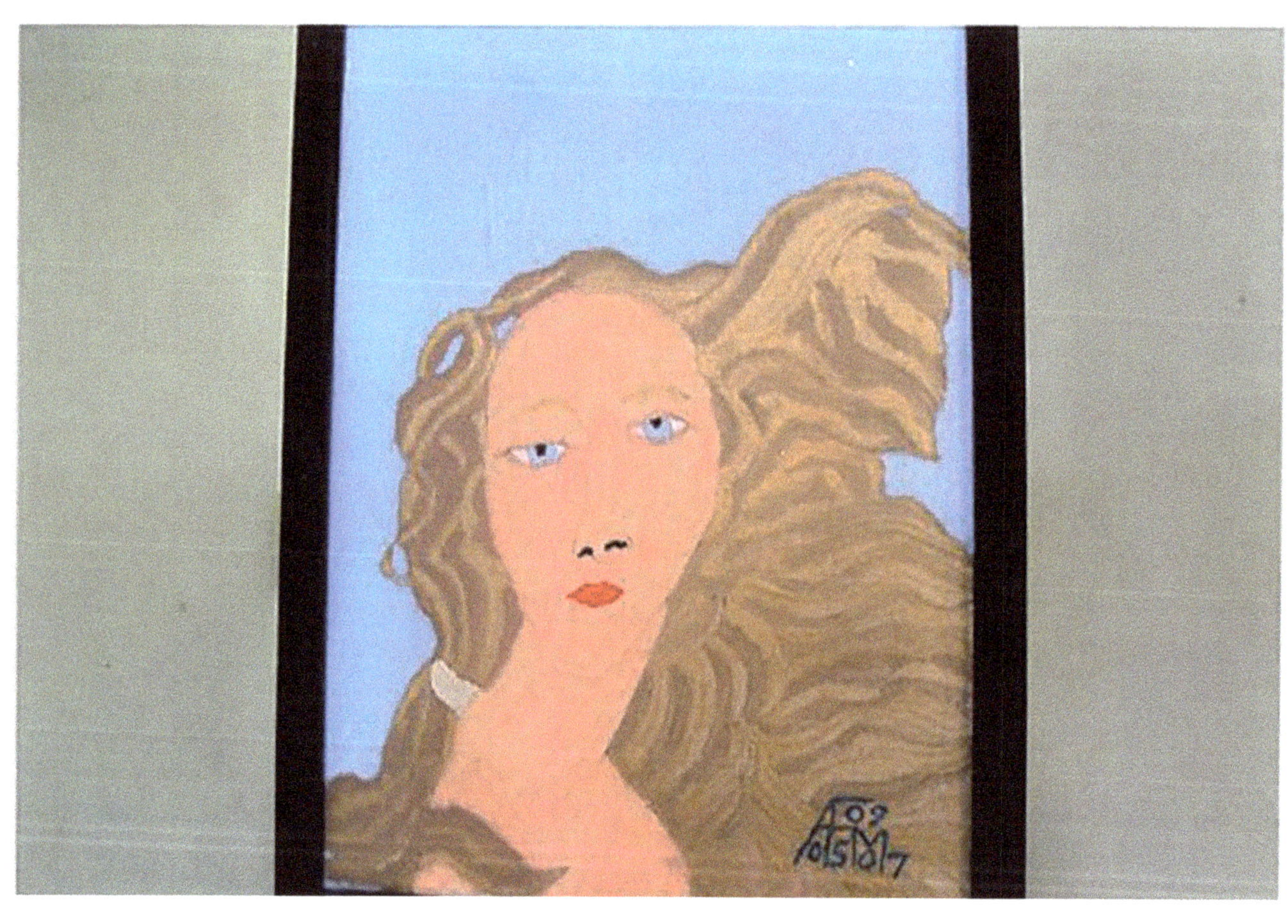

Face of the Botticelli Venus

Rainbow of the Heart

For Judy—

Come with me. I want you
to see the wonder of purple taffeta
Bordered by orange lace trim.

Let me share the rainbow of your
heart in this painting of the singer
in white fringe and sequins.

Anger brightens your works,
signals the party to start.
I am that young American geisha,

A pink field peopled by delicate
flowers on fragile, artfully twisted
branches. Now I dress up

As a really refined lady.
Never fear, it's just another
costume I put on only

For Sunday's reverence.
Expressions come in many
different flavors of feelings.

3/2/93
Revised 11/22/02

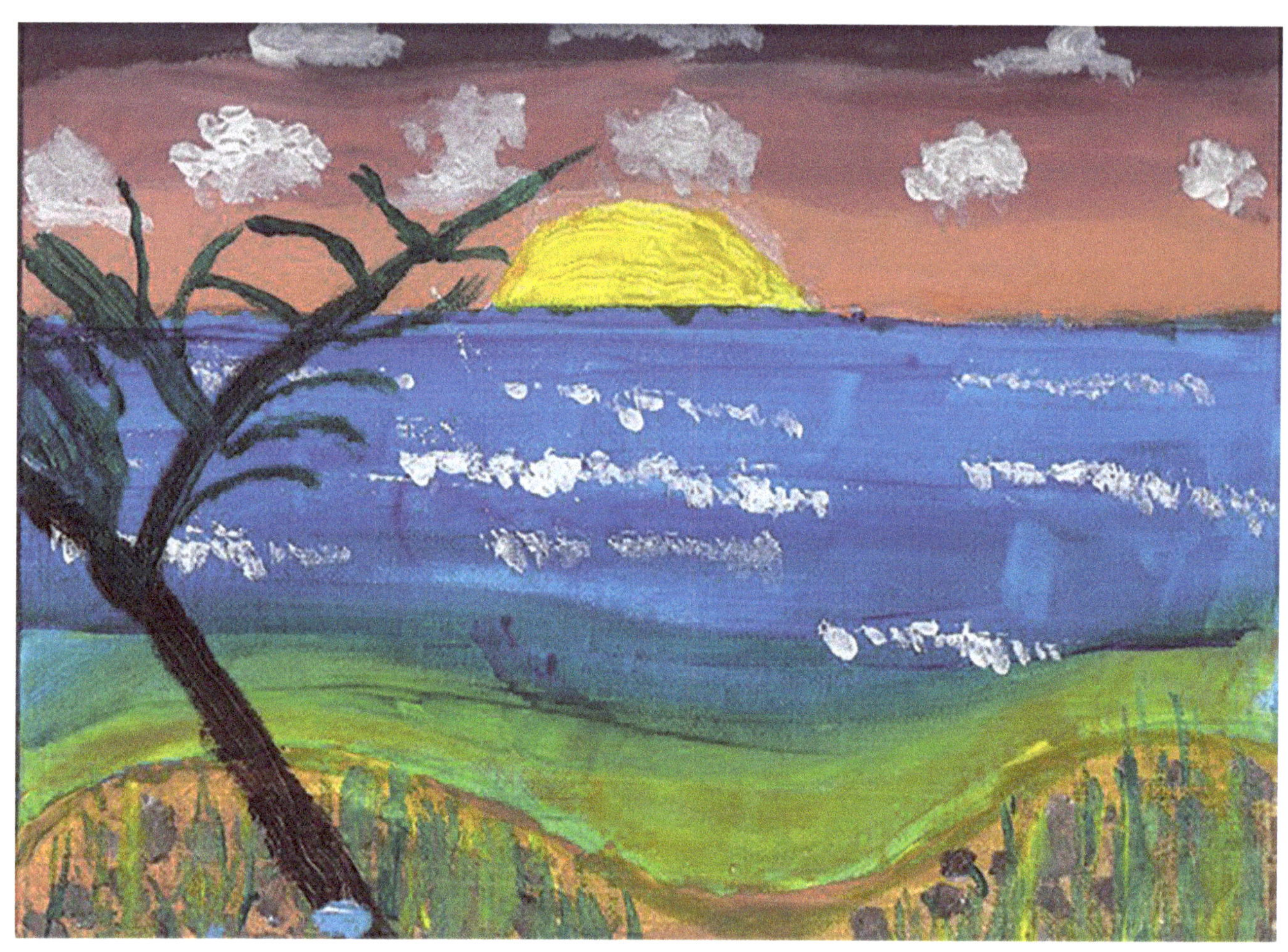

Beachfront Sunrise

Earth Day Redux

Metal and chrome dull,
Scratch the earth of
Broken stone, bottles
And cans crushed under.

Seminars and fact-finding
Discussions create more
Paper on planet's doom to
Be blown-away butterflies.

It is a leaky ship to
Be bailed out before we
Can apply the band-aids.
To abandon is difficult.

Do we have jobs to preserve
Our world before we destroy
The work that wounds us?
At what cost do we rebuild?

We need room to breathe in
Clean rain forests, to find
Mental and physical remedies
While forest lab still stands.

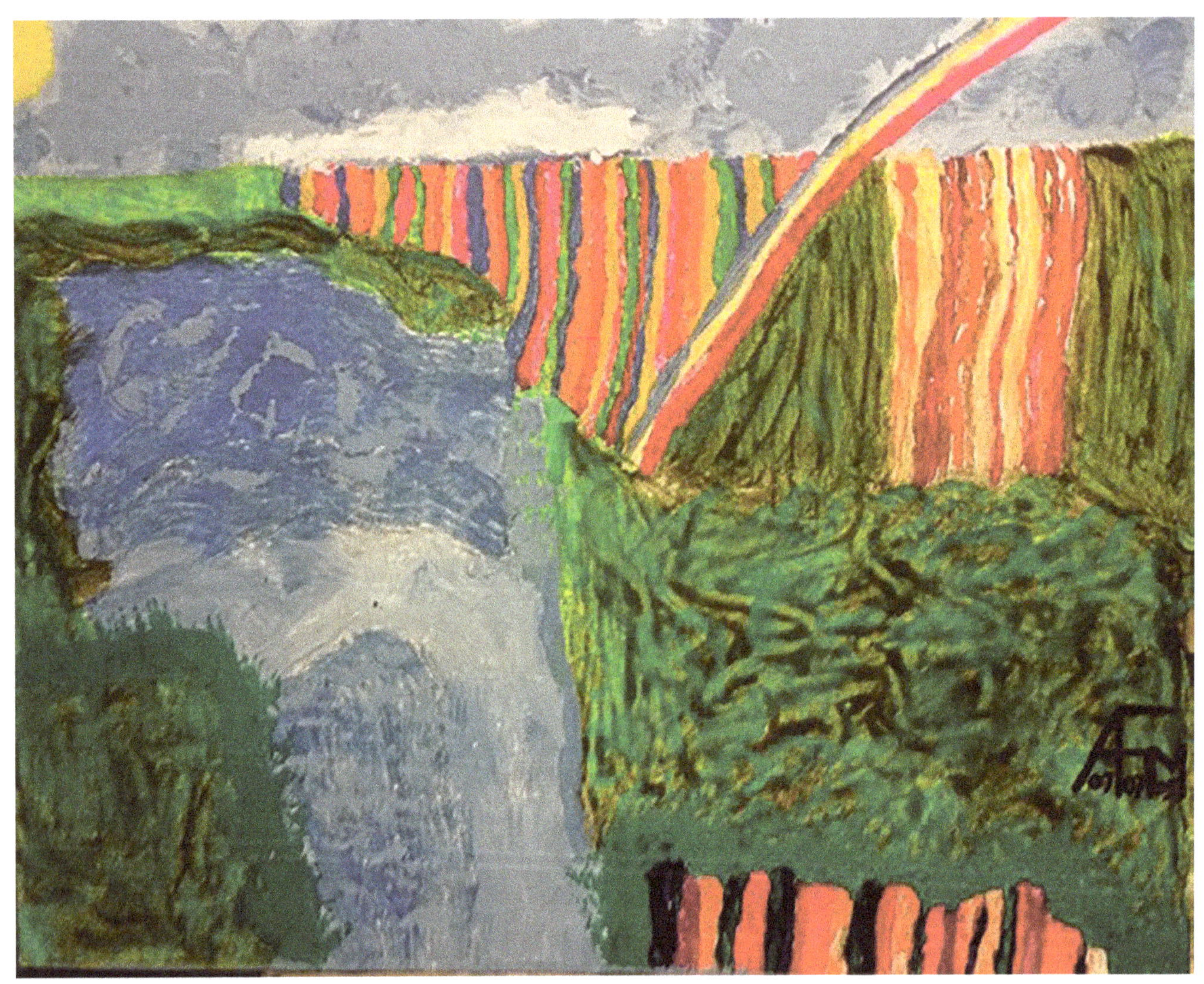

Waterfall Rainbow

Sashes to Sashes

Sashes to sashes, bust to bust.
They see beneath, but never touch—
Their inner treasures, their outer strengths—
The little death of shared pleasure.

They lived together, aged school
Marm and ancient librarian.
Each had dreamed behind closed doors,
Saw the other one in her willing arms.

But neither dared to share more than
Superficial confidences about the men
Whom they never let close.
Each lived within themselves alone.

Love was messy and only to be found
Collectively in books and their titles.
Children were only to be tolerated in
Their place and dared only to grow
Adult in one's dreams.

The two girls, roommates, shopped just
On weekends for clothes and that porcelain
Bird, perfect for their apartment foyer.
The librarian's love letters, the school marm's
Nude studies were found once both had gone.

Revised 12-30-2017

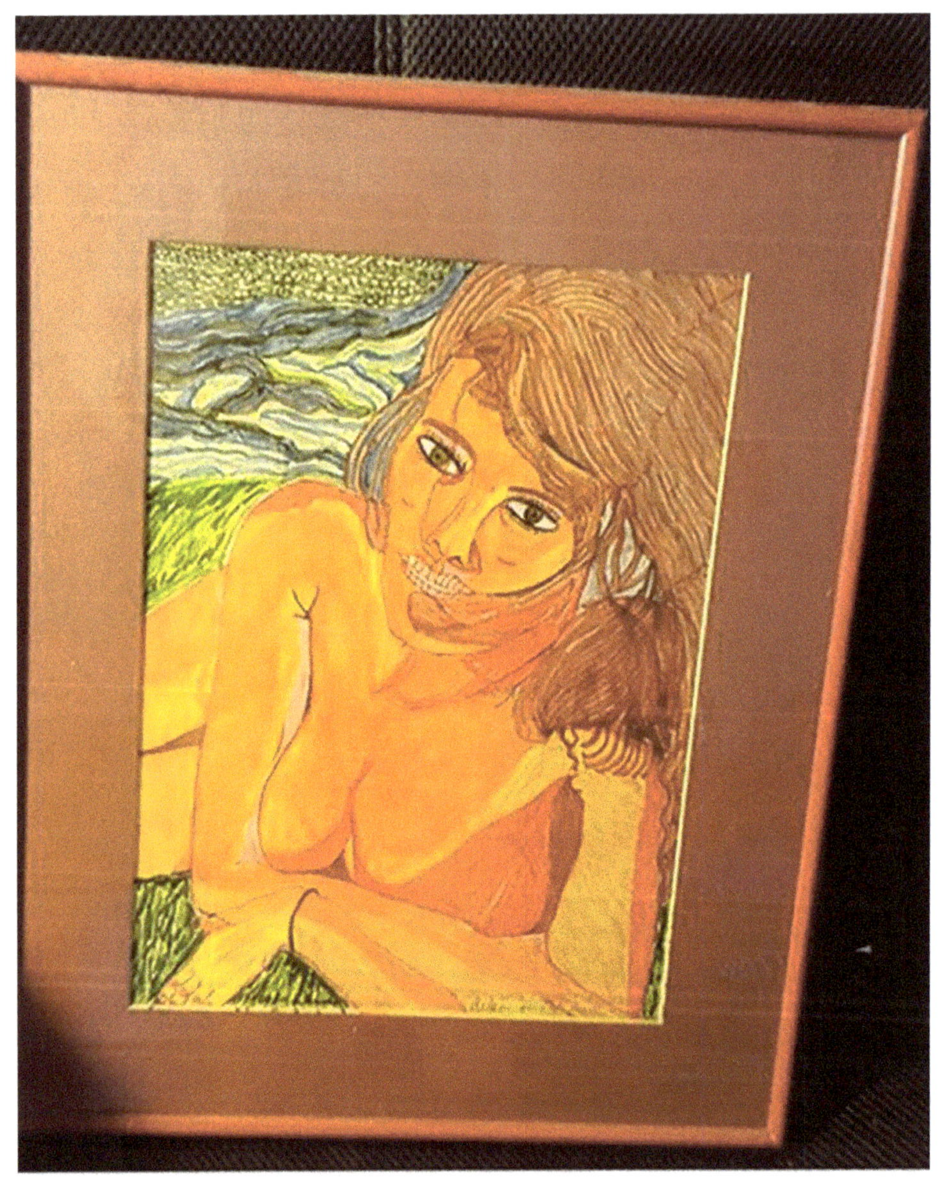

Lady by the Beach

Fresh Pancakes

The slap of your hand
On fresh pancakes,
Warm and finger-hopping good,
Contrasts hotly with
The sting of your words,
Your sickly-sweet comments
About how well I may
Or may not do in life.

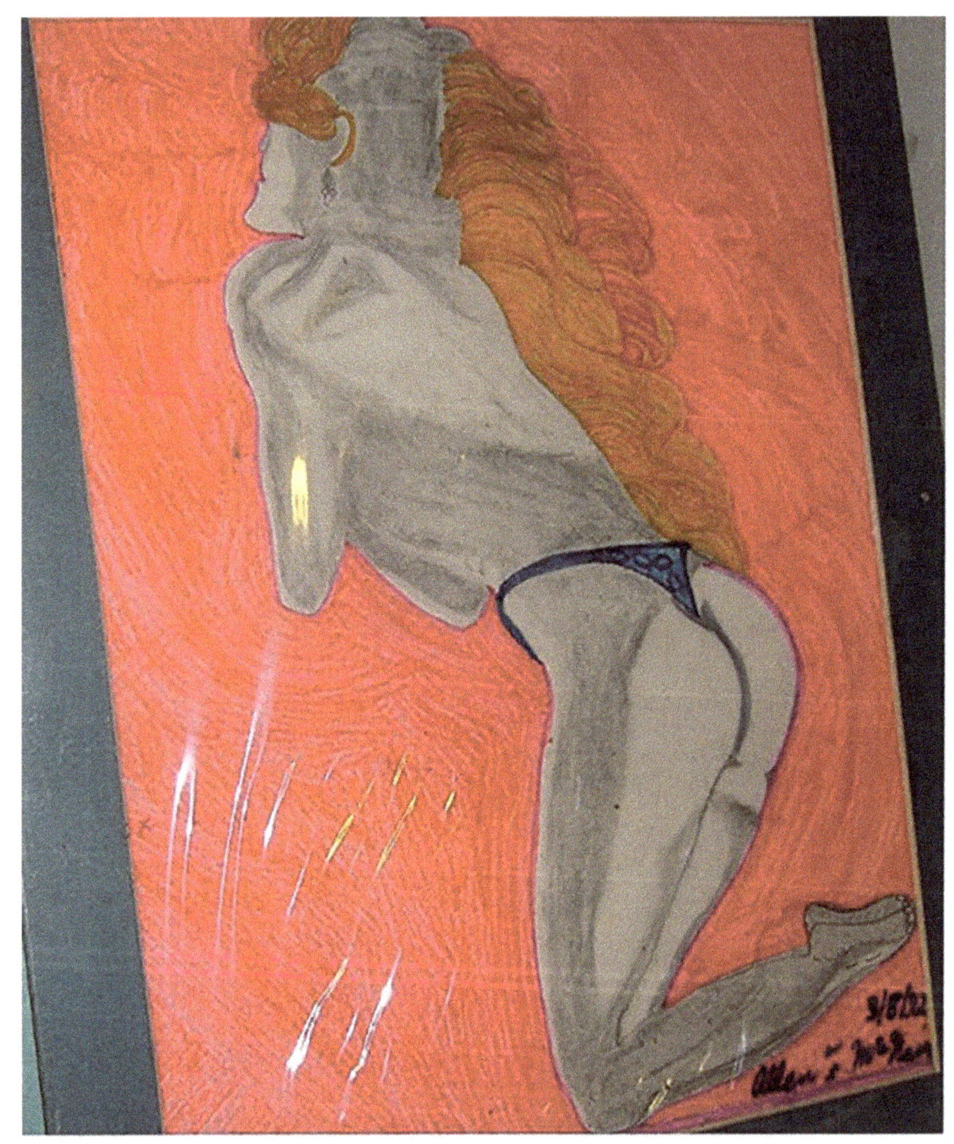

Woman Kneeling

Deep in My Heart, A Little Boy Lives

Deep in my heart
Is emptiness, pain,
There, a little boy lives.
Loud voices in the shadows
Make him wet his pants in fear.
No one comes to change them.

He trips whenever he runs,
His bat misses the ball.
His basketball only hits the rim.
Graceless, coordination never comes.
Lisps color his every sentence—tho what?
His loneliness is often his only friend.

He wants to fight the shadows,
To kill the pain forever.
He wants to calm the loud voices.
Can he smash the pain
From three stories high?
But he is stopped from entering emptiness.

He wants to run everywhere from fear.
Swing his bat to smash the balls of anger.
He wants each basket of plenty and success.
He wants to tear up the loud voices
With as many pills as he can swallow.
But seeks sanctuary from hurting himself.

And I am still alive.

3/24/94

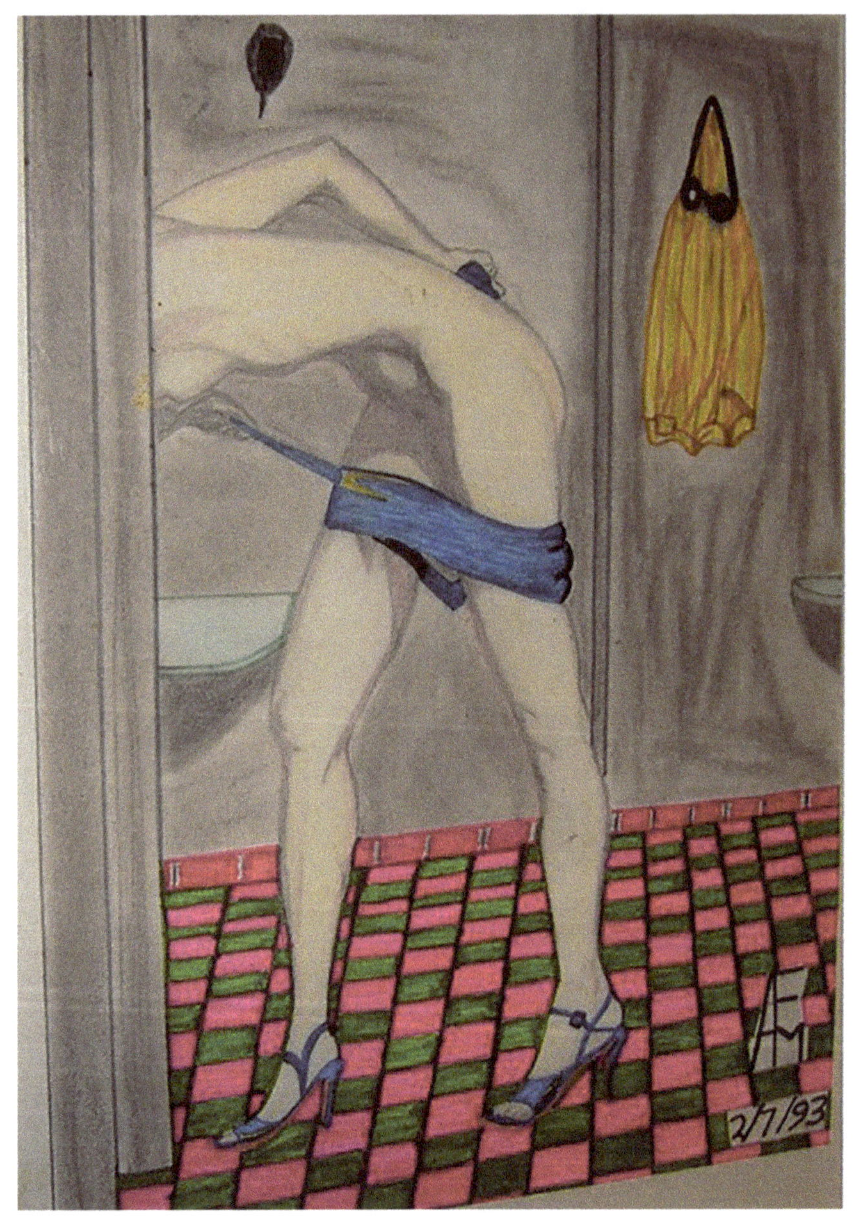

By Her Sink

Between the Human and the Beast

Dripping fangs will surely tear,
as my sharp teeth I bare,
Beware the warning I growl,
as before the moon I howl,
I wasn't always this way,
now, on all fours I play.
Memories vague roam my mind, once I stood from my behind.

Strange is my animal cunning,
while the human mind keeps running.
The person I once knew,
his senses now seem so few.
His smells so often pale,
the hunter must easily fail.
But as I began to change, my awareness has enlarged its range.

Caught between the human and the beast,
fear of the change has become least.
Night images of prowl and chase
rush through my mind space.
Colors flattened to black and white,
yet I thrilled more to my prey's flight.
But as I returned to human form, it felt less like the norm.

The Beast (continued)

Once a woman was attracted to my power,
Our love a fragrant flower.
She understood my transformation,
we strengthened our relation.
Then between us arose a great foe,
victim of my bite, he grows
Stronger in evil, destruction, he increases in corruption.

The battle ferocious, I am victorious,
dead is the one malicious.
Now, the wild calls most powerful,
I can't resist its strong pull.
To now protect my true love,
away humanity I shove.
Long and fast my purposeful strides, into deep forest now I hide.

02/01/95

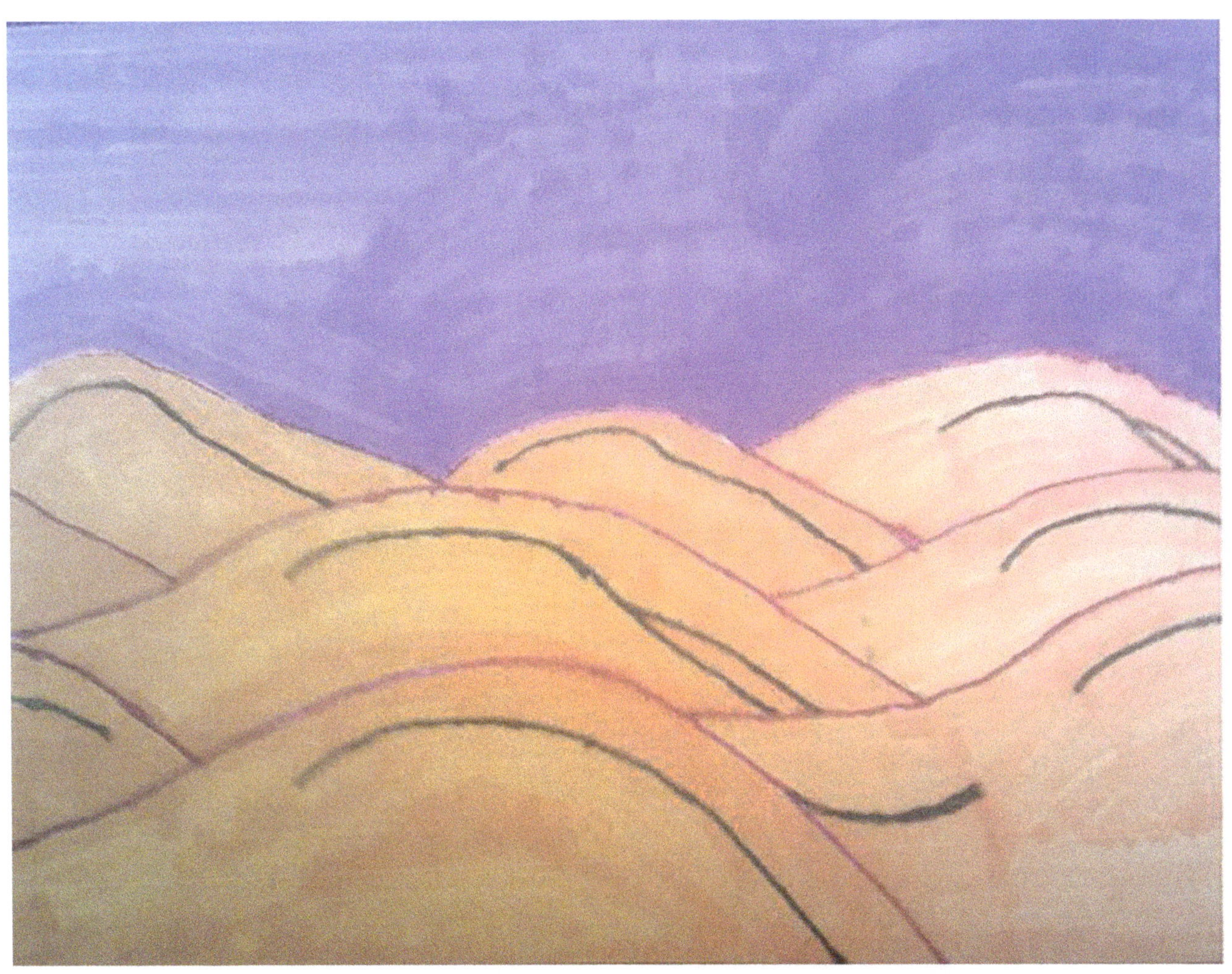

Human Wave II

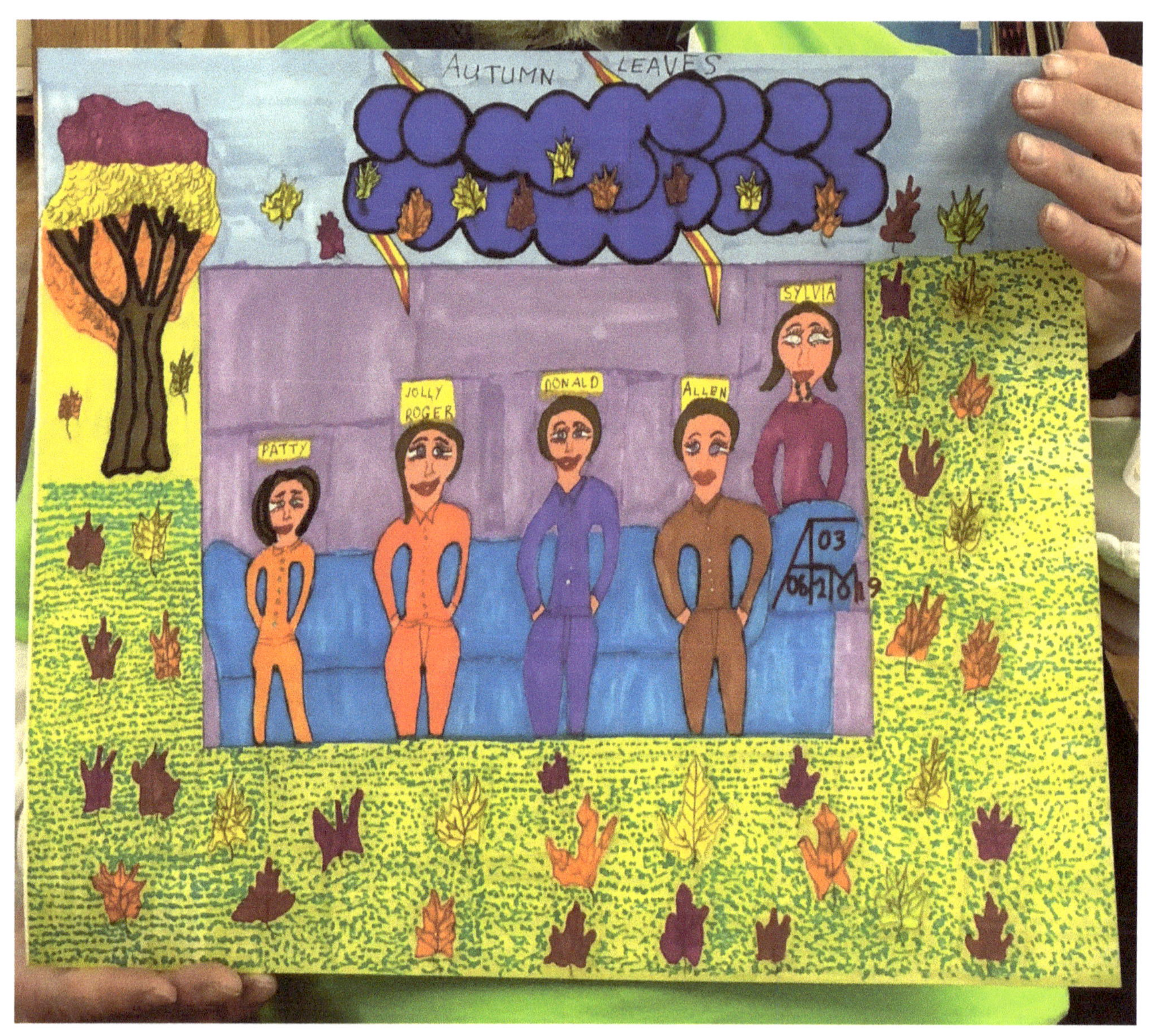

Autumn Leaves
(2019-13-03)

Autumn Leaves

The autumn leaves whip past my window,
Scattered in circles, fallen
From the trees of our indifference.
The voices in the other room too loud.

Mom is crying, Dad still shouts.
But we must look outside at the leaves,
The different colors, we watch the deep greens
Turned to oranges, dark reds, yellows.

The outside leaves color our confusion,
Our various moods circle among them.
Why does Daddy stumble inside?
Hover over us, breathing heavily?

His smiles are false, his words sting.
We turn away to look outside,
To let the slap of words, fly away
On circling, multicolored leaves.

Mamma, come look at the autumn leaves.
Let Daddy find his bed to sleep.
Watch the leaves circle with our feelings.
Let them carry the sting away of our pain.

02/14/95

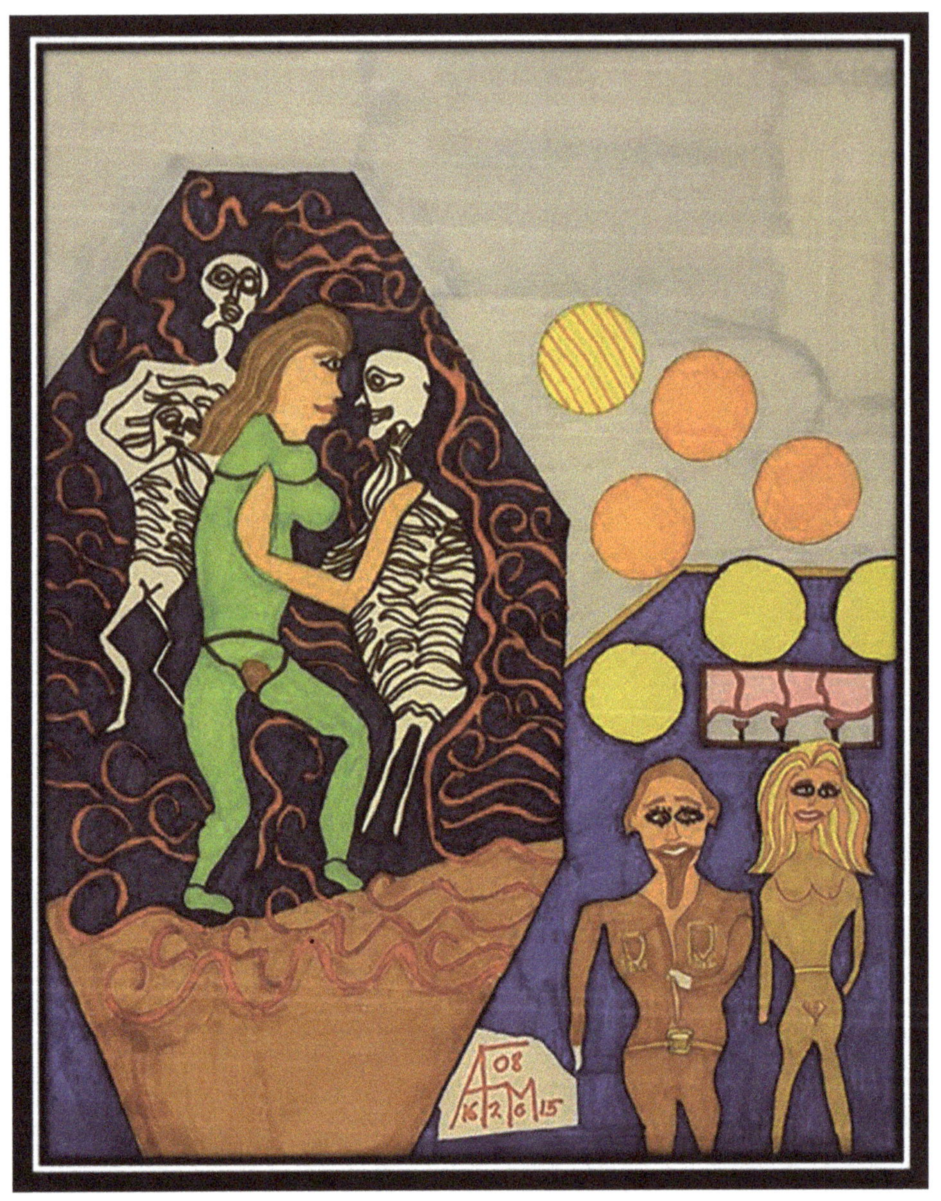

Blackest Night of Each One's Horror

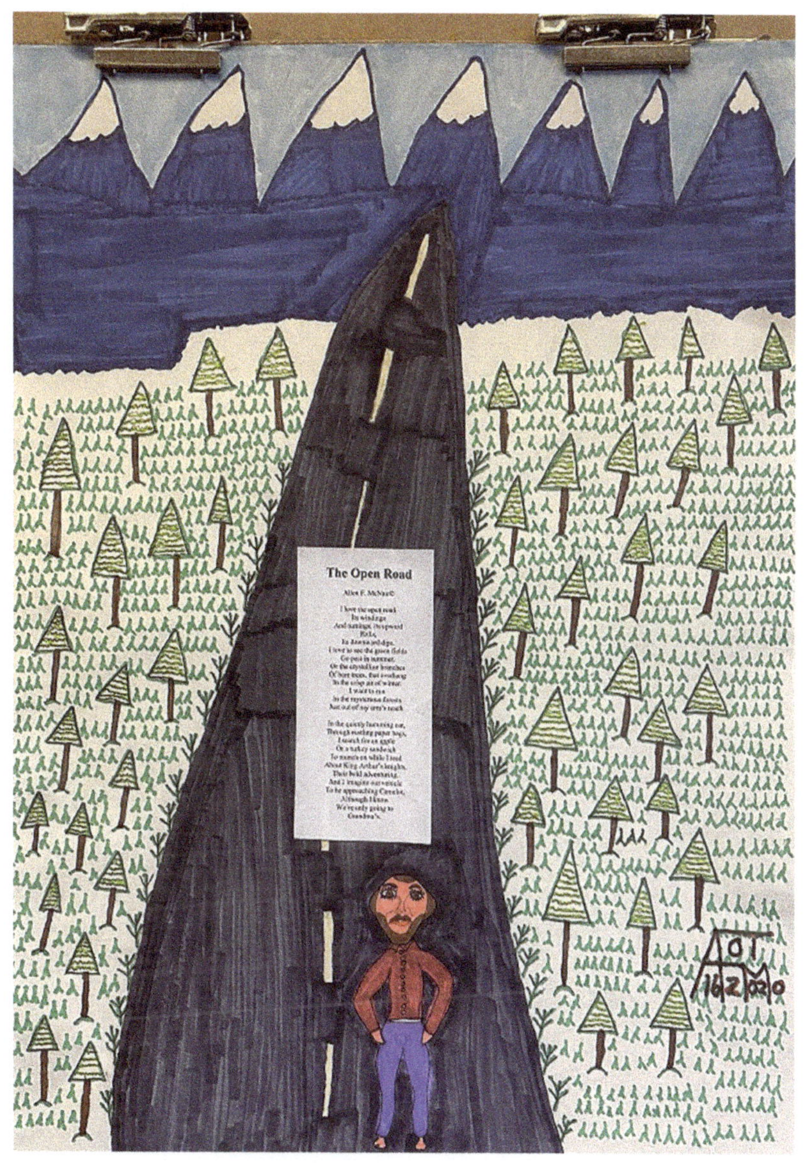

The Open Road Painting with Poem
(2020-01-16)

The Open Road

I love the open road.
Its windings
And turnings, its upward
Rolls,
Its downward dips.
I love to see the green fields
Go past in summer,
Or the crystalline branches
Of bare trees, that overhang
In the crisp air of winter.
I want to run
In the mysterious forests
Just out of my arm's reach.

In the quietly humming car,
Through rustling paper bags,
I search for an apple
Or a turkey sandwich
To munch on while I read
About King Arthur's knights,
Their bold adventuring,
And I imagine our vehicle
To be approaching Camelot,
Although I know
We're only going to
Grandma's.

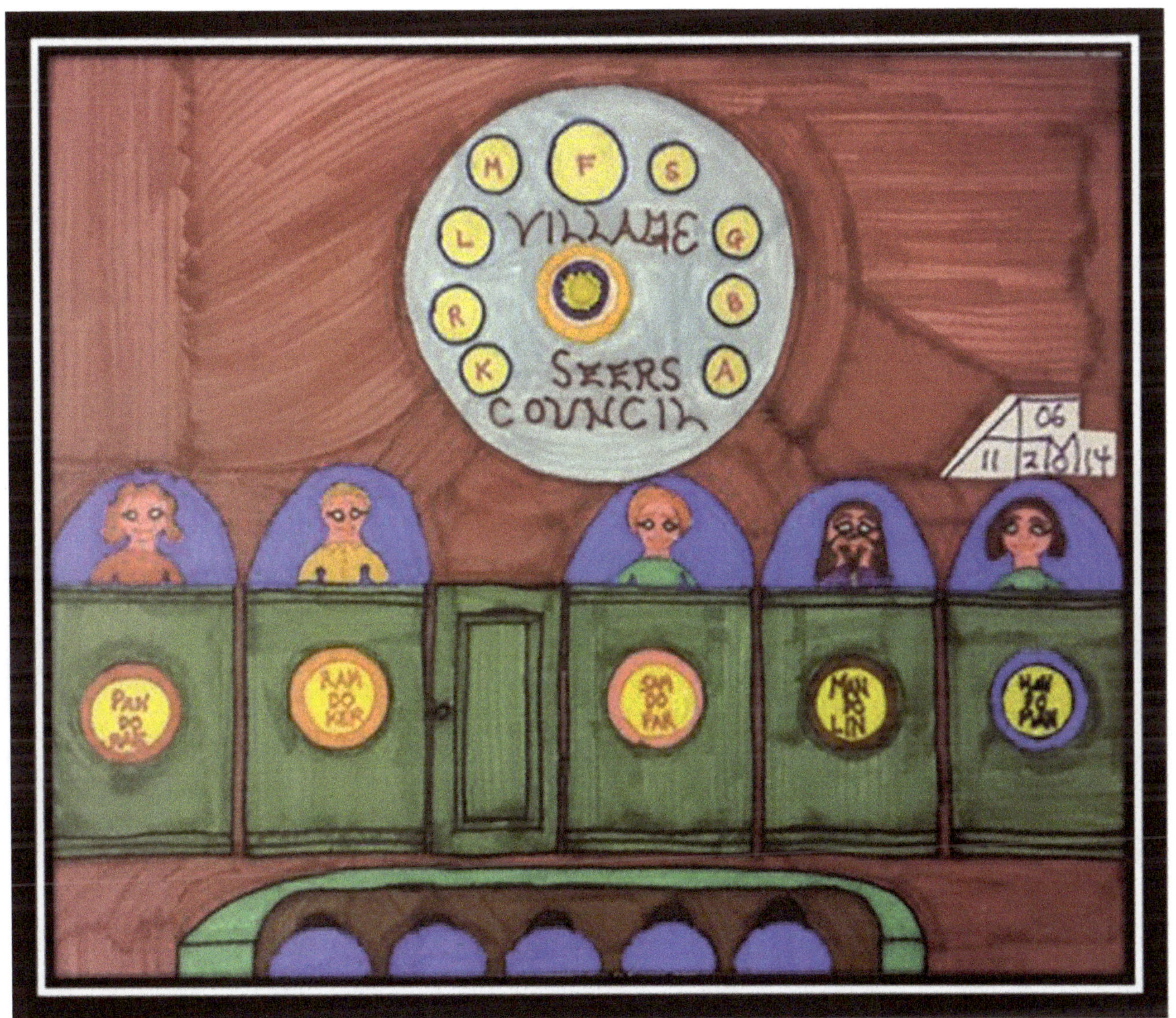

Yet Humble and Wise

Too Brief a Candle

Chance meeting on well-lit street
I saw a blonde angel
Who spoke of parties and new pantyhose

We remembered last encounter
Among the bright people
Who help the nameless

How busy life sometimes becomes
Among poor and well-off alike
Fresh excitements quickly stale

Pleasure is all too brief a candle
To always catch its flickering light
You had to go, as did I

Suddenly become tired, I promised
To be in touch
We embraced in parting

I can only hope in the future
We know which
Promises to keep.

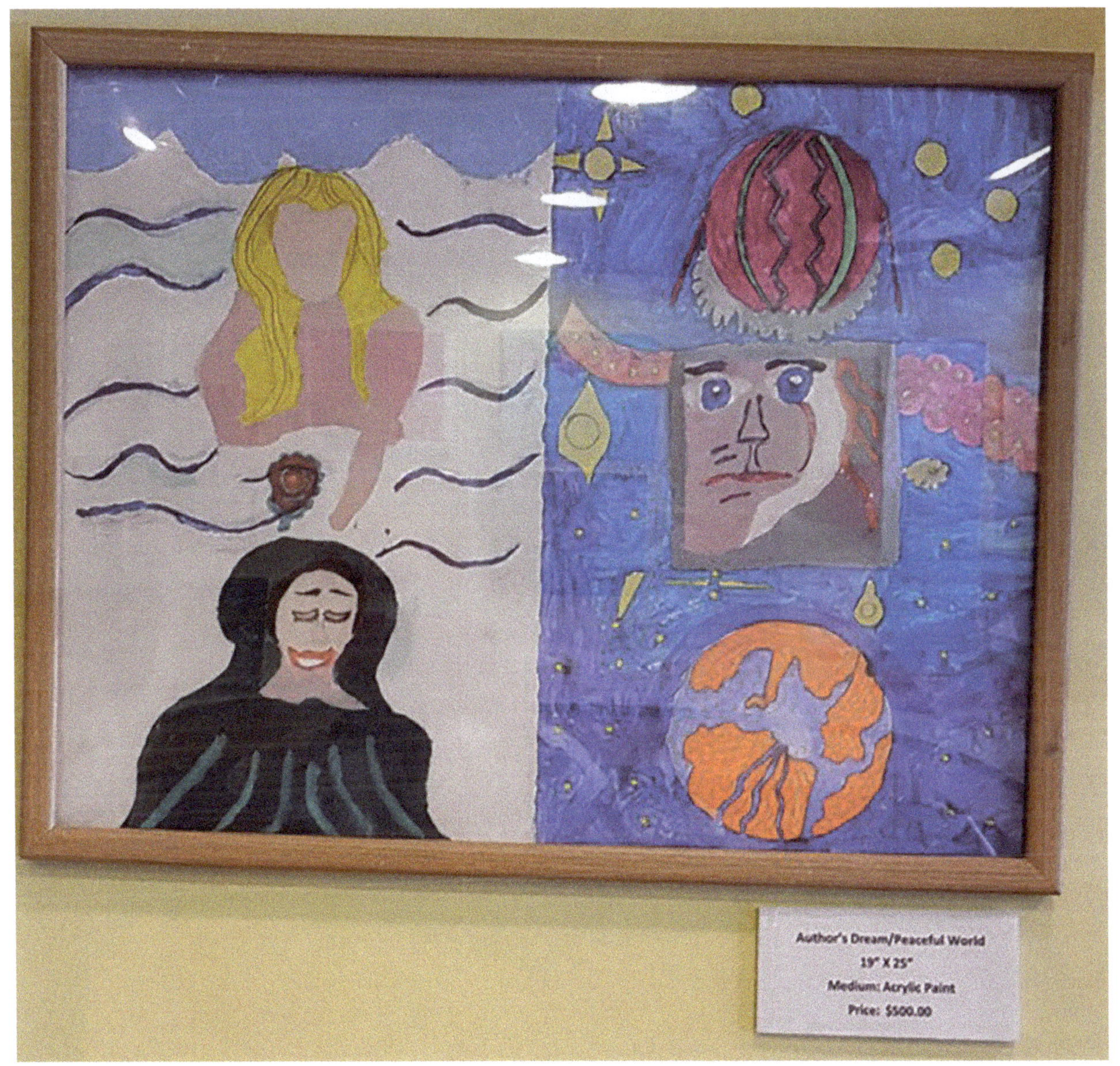

Author's Dream/Peaceful World

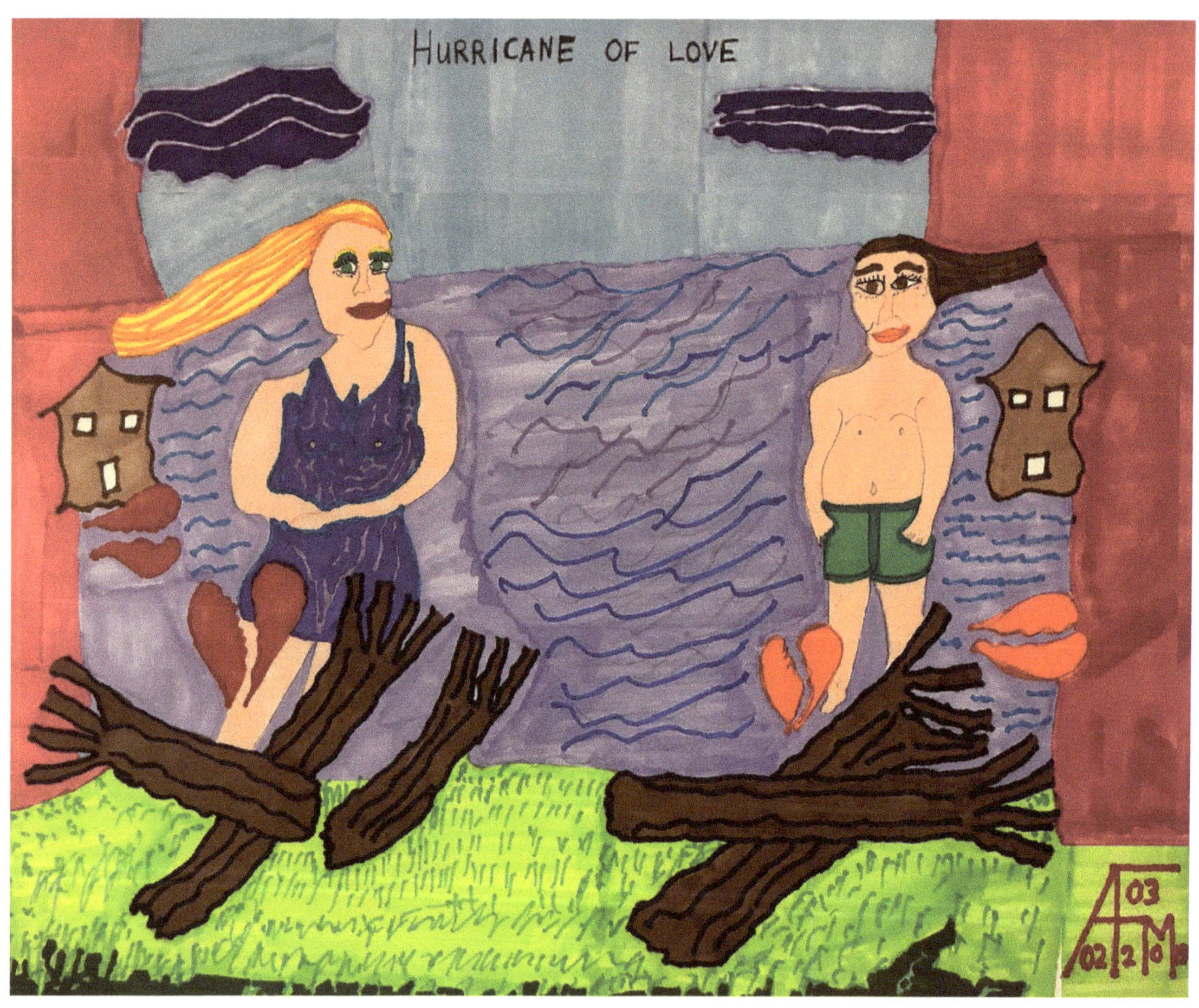

Hurricane of Love
(2019-06-03)

Hurricane of Love

The hurricane of love blasts away
All reason to play it safe.
I can't hold back my confession
Of feelings so intense, a barrier
Rises between us, places an immediate
Distance before our friendship.

Once a perfect island of calm approval,
Our stronghold of well-earned trust.
All the sheltering trees leveled,
Now so many toothpicks;
Our grass hut of comfort
Lashed apart by winds conflicting.

What seemed so clear to me when I felt
The tidal inrush of affection for you,
Becomes muddied by your tepid response.
I have traveled this road sufficiently
To know the edge well enough not to fall
Off every time someone new comes into my life.

But when a tender wave carries me,
I become foolhardy to push friendship
Toward furthest shores of romance,
Intimacy, on quietly towards commitment.
What am I doing so wrong
That I cannot have my wish?

I can't stop this feeling of my love.
I cast forth my loving net
For your tender heart.
If it's caught within
Those gentle strands on water,
I patiently await its return.

09/30/91
Revised 01/27/96

You Fantastic Mouse!

Oh! You're a fantastic mouse—
The sorcerer's apprentice.
You and I are a lot alike.
One day I thought to avoid
A chore of removing my trash.

When I asked a friend to do it, he asked me
What I would do for him in exchange.
I thought and pondered what would suit
Someone who is adult in age,
Yet child-like in mind and temperament.

Candy, I didn't have, my usual art-work
Too mature for simple enjoyment.
Then I remembered a little mouse
From days of silver screen, who
Delighted both young and old.

We loved his magic movements,
Fascinated by his pure comedy.
Could I draw a favorite character
Of my childhood innocence?
Or am I now too jaded by life?

Fantastic Mouse! (continued)

Am I too cynical by my adult experience?
Now I was more determined to prove
I was otherwise.
Then you, fantastic mouse, came forth
From your picture to my pen and marker.

High on your mountain ledge, a wave of
Your hand directs the very stars of
Your magical kingdom.
My world then changed for the better, too.
You and I seem to become new friends.

As I pester people to make comment
On my drawing, I quickly realize
That my child/adult friend cannot know
Nor understand what real value—
For cheer or laughter—you give to many.

I repay my young friend's helpfulness
With small change, instead.
Next, I look for another place to
Showcase my vision of your magic form.

Fantastic Mouse! (continued)

I show you to my skin doctor, who
Has also viewed my playful women
On the bright beaches, the tender
Ones lounging in the boudoir.
She liked them, but you catch her eye.

A project forms—my comic pictures
On her clinic's walls!
Enlarged and framed!
Cheerful colors for children
Scared of doctors, hospitals.

Cartoon characters, behind colored
Paper and clear glass.
Clowns, little pet kittens.
Cats and playful puppy dogs,
Come play with waiting kids.

Whose turn to be examined next?
So, went my first sale, you and
Four other friends were soon sold.
I owe it to you, my most fantastic mouse.

06/05/94
Revised 01/27/95

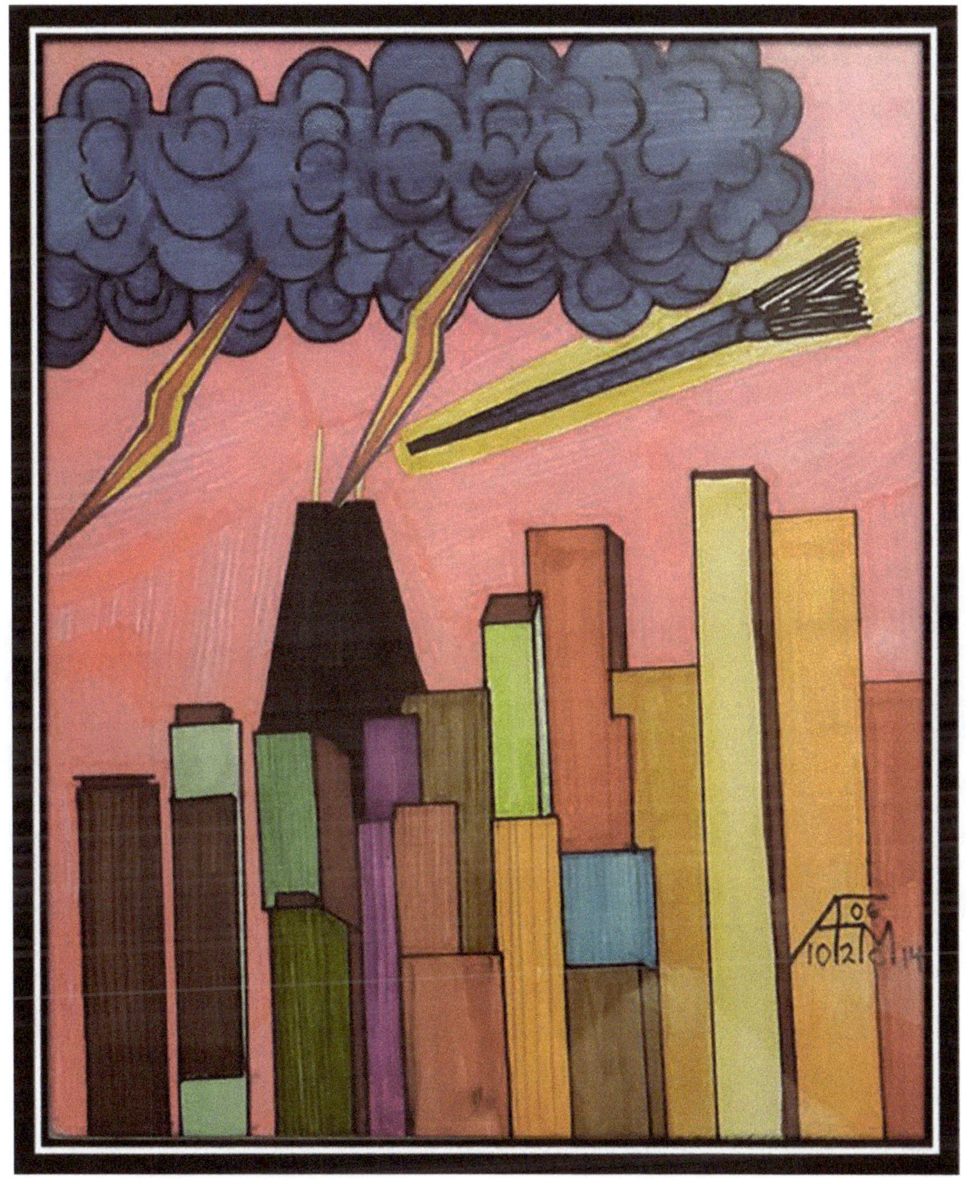

Flying Engines Thunder Close

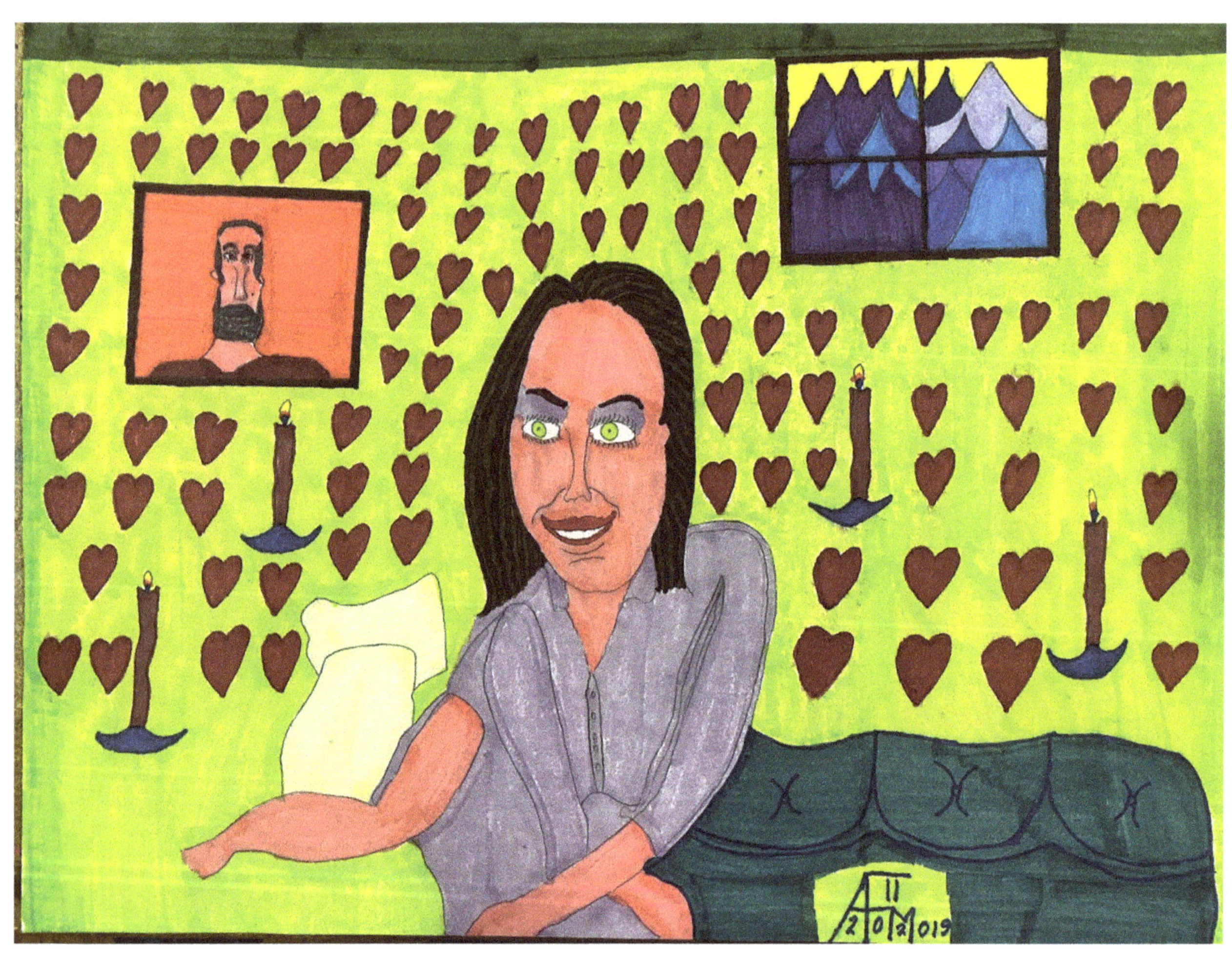

Your Face in Candlelight
(2019-11-15)

Your Face in Candlelight

Your face I see in candlelight
Reflects a mystery not bound by time
Your eyes express limitless space.
Two stars of passion which burn.

The night sky flows through your hair.
The river of night runs between my fingers.
Your cheeks are soft as silk.
Yet fine as sculpted marble.

I love your very lips.
Lush as sweetest cherries.
Yet touching mine, I am lifted
By fireworks tearing at my soul.

You spark my greatest imagination.
Deep inside, I am burned alive.
Beneath rough flannel, your heart beats
To the rise and fall of tender breast.

In mind and soul, we are united.
Your love and mine the same.
And the day that I will meet you,
I'll see your face in candlelight.

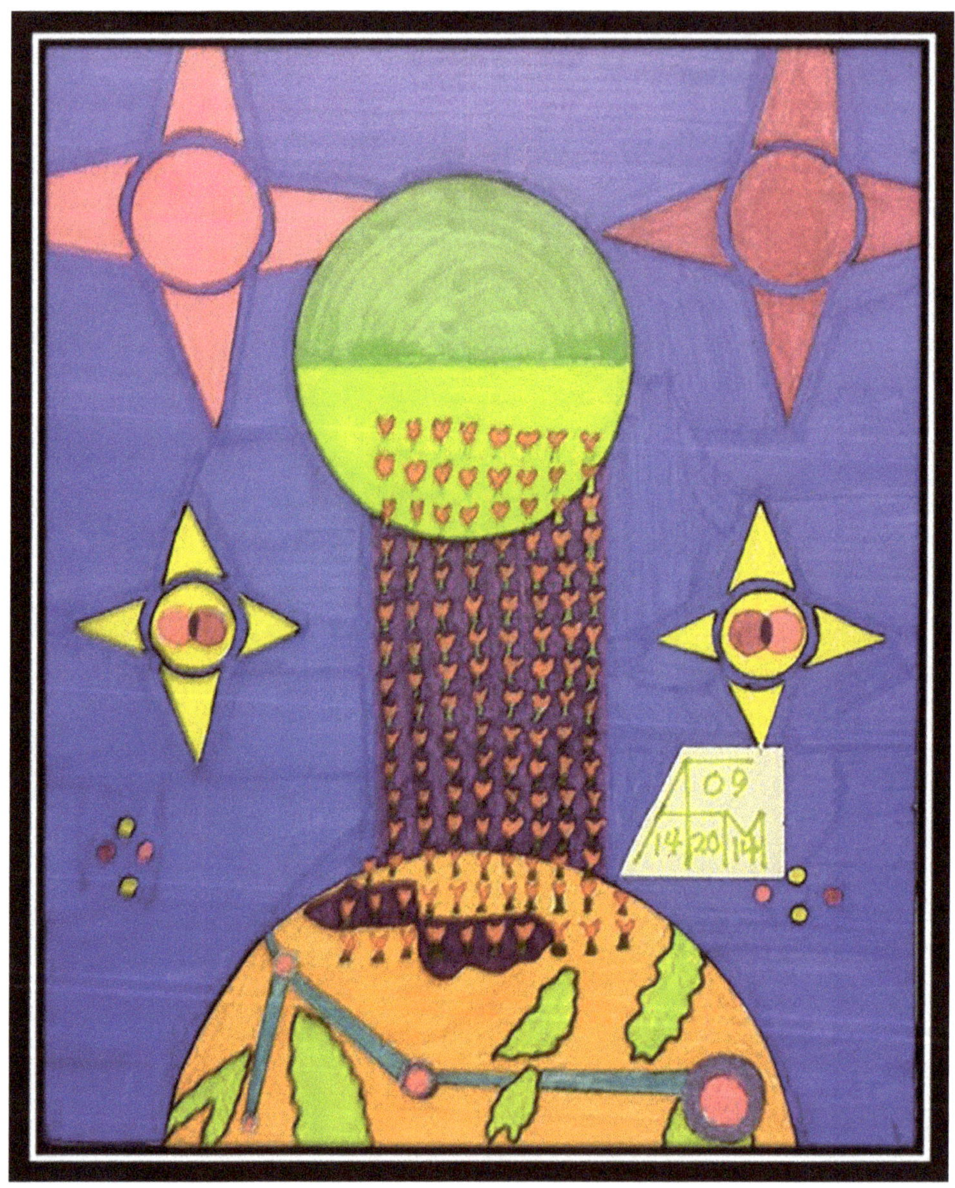

Alien Flowers Travel through Space

Of Silver Thoughts

Dead fish dream
Of silver thoughts.
They float
Inside my head.

Chocolate orange peels
Twist and writhe
Within my bloodstream,
My denizens of desire.

Sirens scream
In sweet songs
Of tragedy and
Sometimes life prolonged.

Abstract foolishness
In concrete illusions
The baby's cry hurts
And lunacy babbles on.

In the emergency room,
I return to the womb.
I float from the pain
Of life's poking, prodding.

Drum beats, heart beats.
Feet rise and fall
In patterns of dance.
Life is joyous in rhythm.

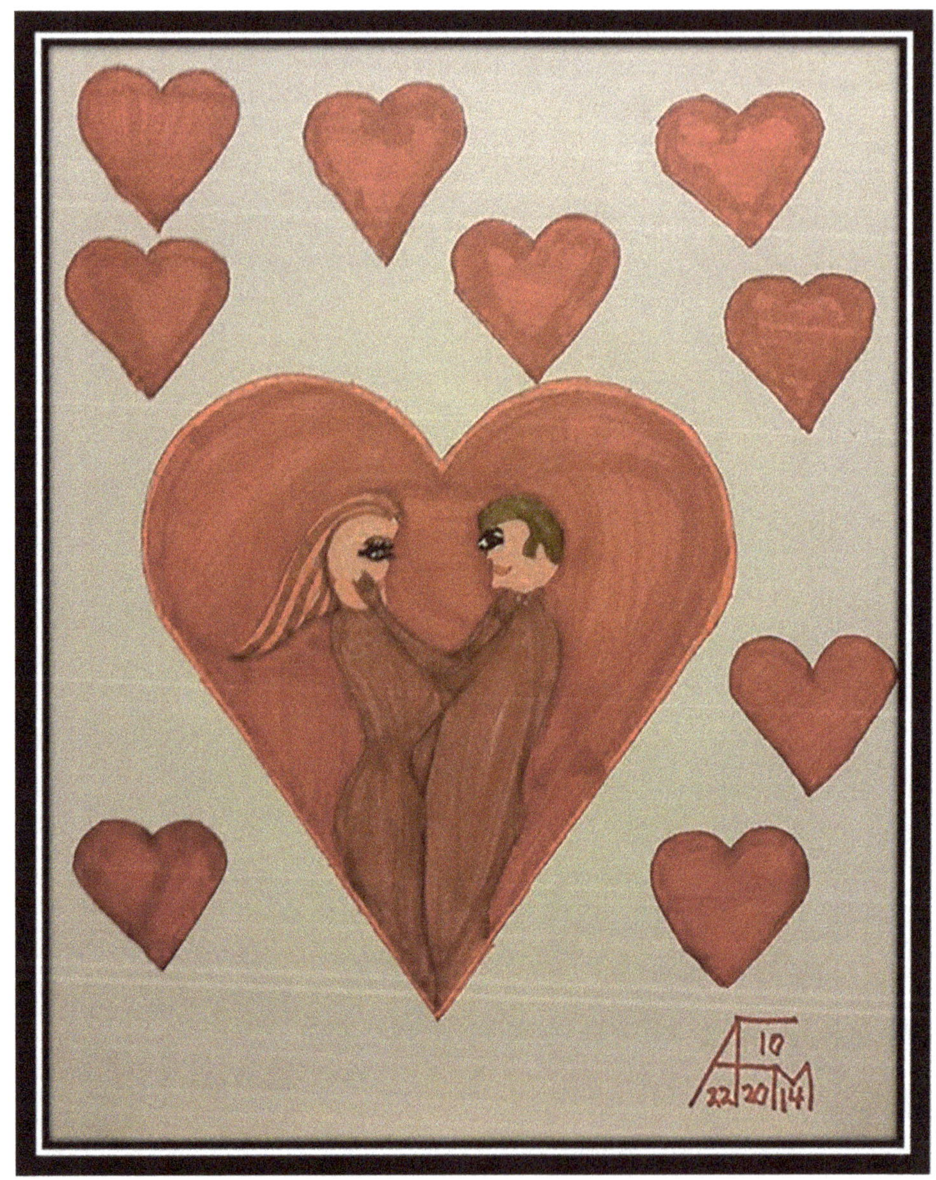

A New Couple in Love

The Midwest Farmer

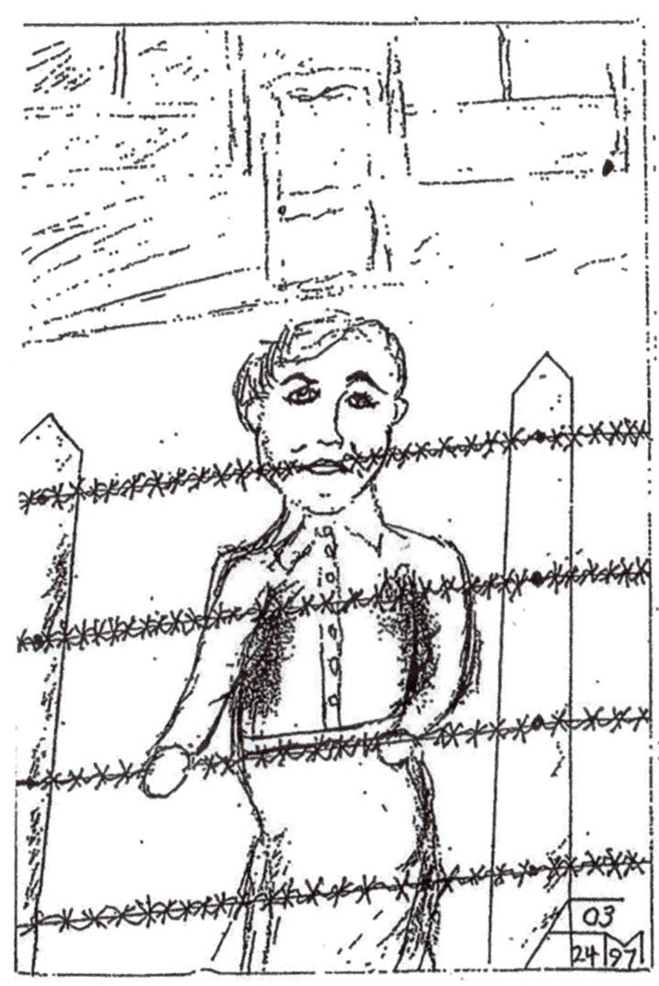

He is a tall, reed of a man.
His balding gray wisps of hair
Frame a mind of wit and wisdom.
Seeming innocent, he sees all.

Farmer (continued)

Midwest farmer, he lived past
Both ample springs and stingy,
Wet and dry, lazy summers hot,
Bountiful and sickly fall harvests.

Weathered by cold, silent winters,
He fathered three hardy sons with
Human discipline as harsh, as
Relentless as their environment.

Like a true Scotsman, he could
Make a penny scream the way
A lone wolf howls at the moon
On a cold, dark friendless night.

Their hearts were weak, first to
Fall was his eldest son: years
After, his second left this earth.
His heart weakened by the bottle.

Sober and smokeless throughout
His life, he always questioned
Whether his second son's family
Fell prey to cigarettes, alcohol.

This photo is at odds with my kind
Image of his aged father,
My Dad grew into adulthood—
Did his father show any kindness?

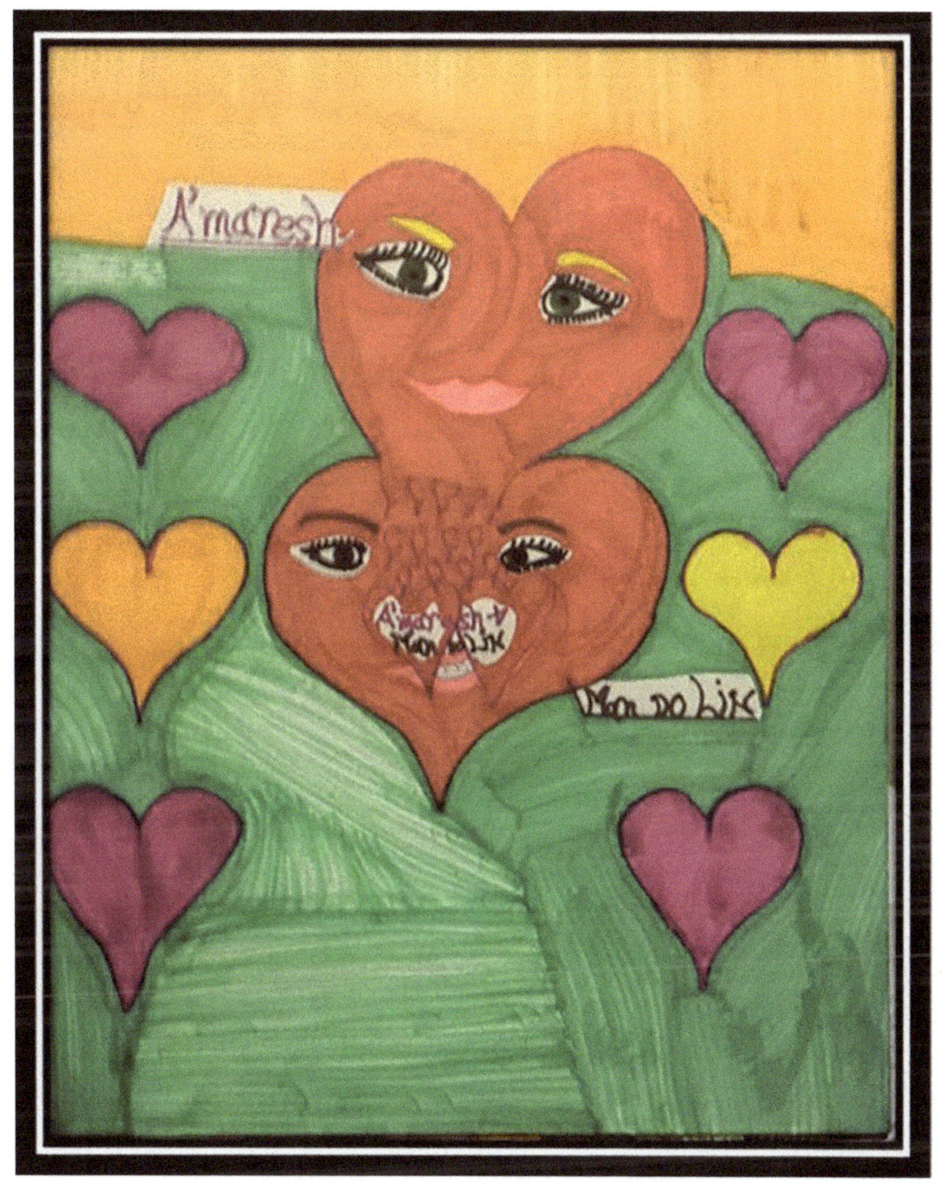

Her Heart Melts into His

Glass of Life

The heart swells and soars
At the very sight of you.
I want for nothing more
When I am with you.

Your smile is my pleasure,
So ruby red and white.
Your laugh is filled with you.
Eyes shine emerald in the night.

Your voice is wild water,
My thirst is all ways slaked.
In a desert far away,
I feel my poor heart ache.

Your figure is an hourglass,
The bright sands count the time,
Of every hour we spend,
So precious, you are mine.

My happy heart is open
To every joy you bring.
Our love is a sweet pink rose,
In the glass of life, it springs.

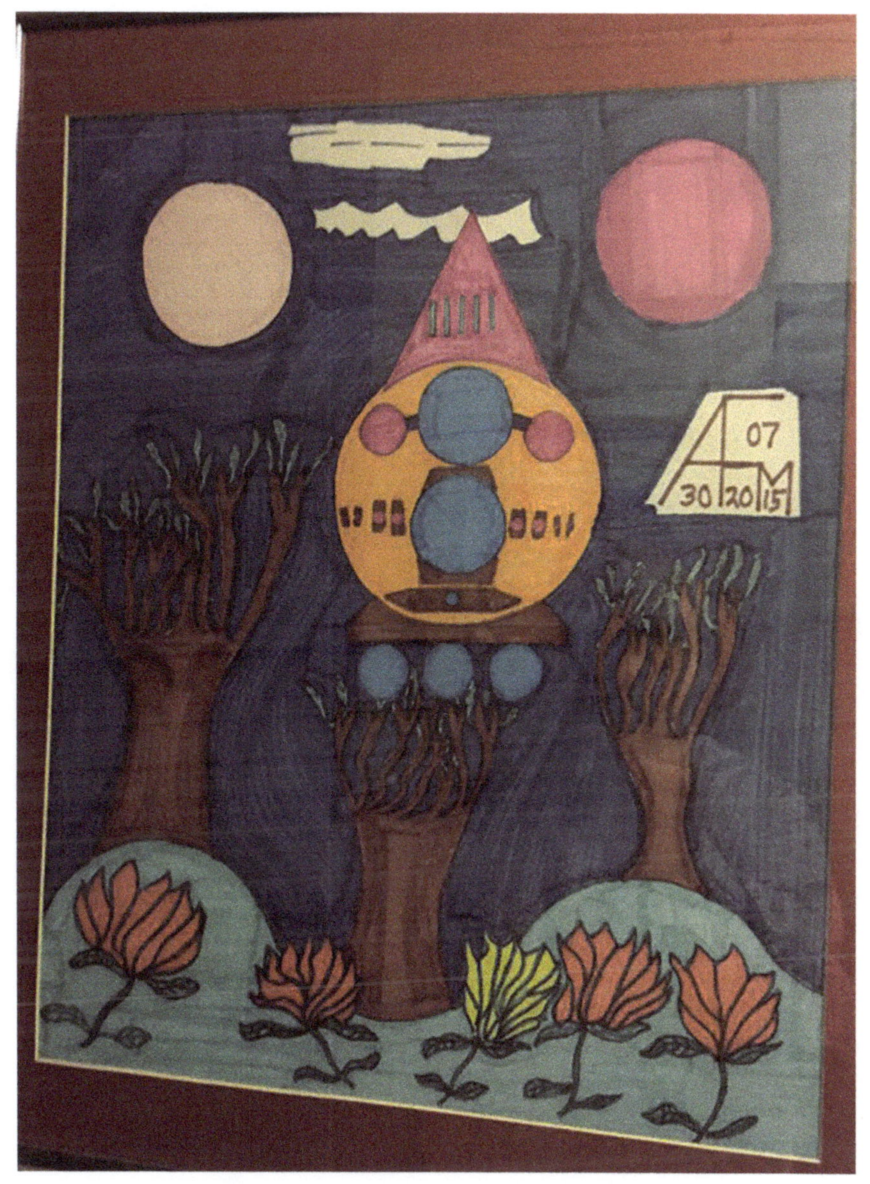

Carpet of Woods and Flowers

Hidden Dance

For Annie—

The music charges through her limbs
To wrap around her heart an
Opens it to those memories
Of someone not there.

Her laugh comes to her ear
As a ghost of his caring.
Her feet move as if
To reach across

The closed miles apart.
His arms, not there,
Encircle her shoulders.
She feels the pattern

Of his clothes in her arms.
On that hidden dance floor
Within her, he dances.
Her smile that touches

All around her is actually
Meant for him alone.
The music throws itself at her
Just the way he would rush into her.

06/01/96

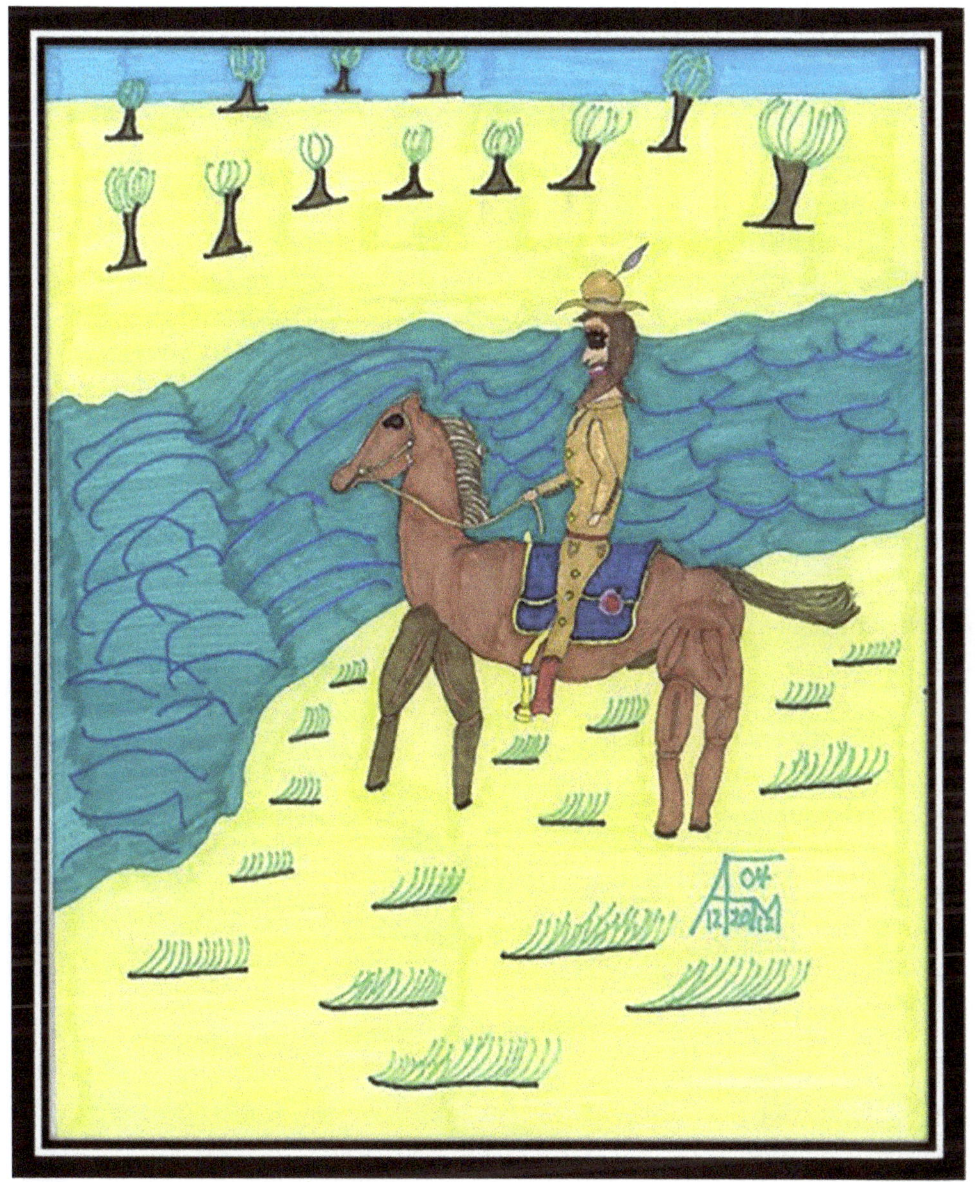

By Clear, Cool Pool

My Two Worlds

I live in two worlds. The
First is one of accomplishment,
Of college degree and literary
Talent readily acknowledged.

The other is of abject poverty and
Cold, thoughtless residence, of
Shelter filled with unknown men
And careless, heartless agencies.

In the past, I looked out of
A warm-lit clothing store
To see a ragged woman—she
Seemed as distant as the moon.

My first world is of brightly colored
Books and new clothes not yet worn.
It speaks of money and belonging.
But I retreat from it, apart from it

And join the army of walking wounded,
The untapped potential of the real people
Who walk the bombed-out streets beside
The false display of life's riches.

While I rebuild the first world,
My heart remains open to bring
Along the real people I've met
Into my future dreams and yours.

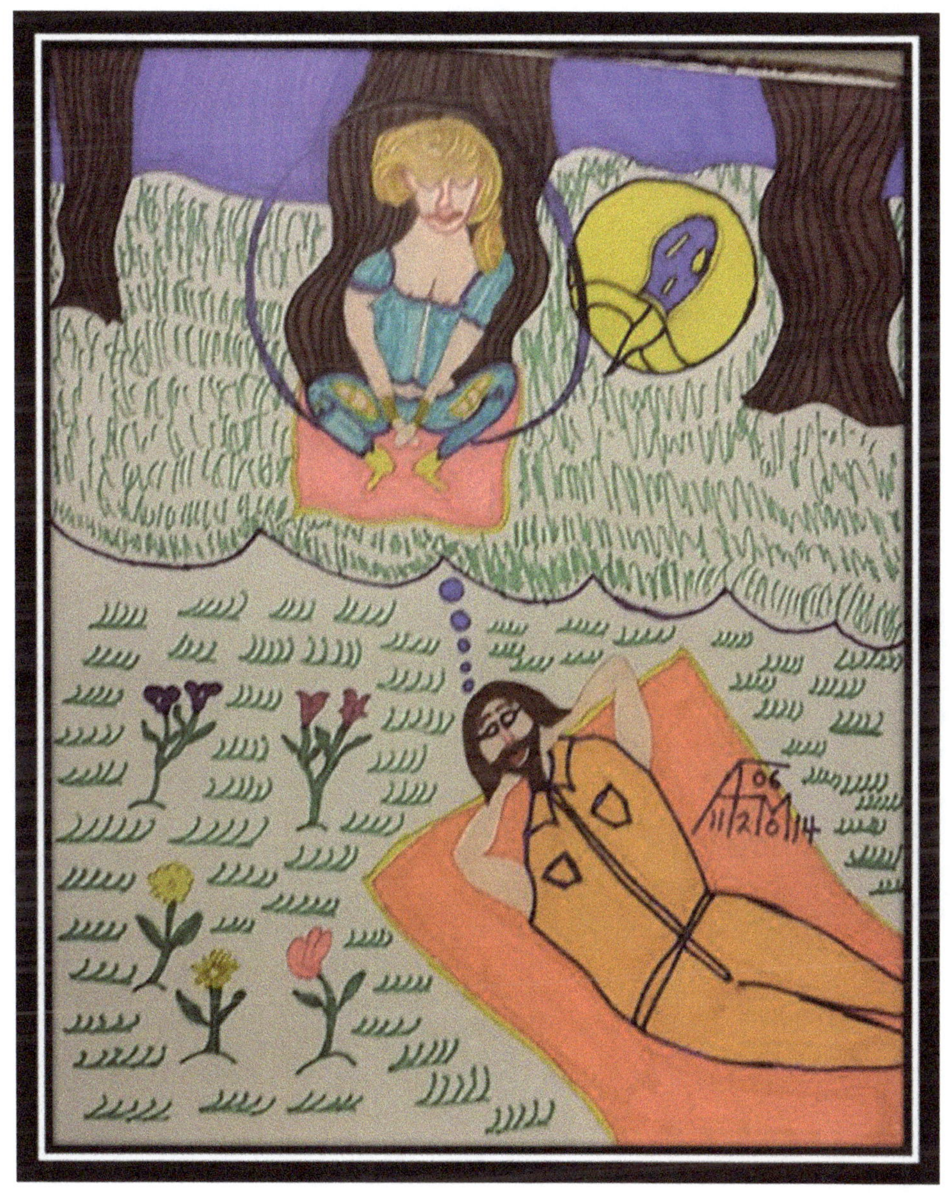

At Night Asleep

Sultry Ice

Scarlet curtain of
Comfortable curves
Draped on piano, her
Smile is sultry ice.

Black, rippled mirror
Of fine polished wood
Shows reflected ghost
Of beauty's mystery.

A languid waterfall over
Piano's front, her hand
Holds still slow music
Slow and ragtime sheets.

Black tie and formal gown
Mix with couples in casuals,
The crowd is a smoky blur
Through eyes clouded by curls.

Throaty songs and sensual, her
Voice caresses her listeners.
Raw notes reach into foot's
Arch, magic hands on her hips.

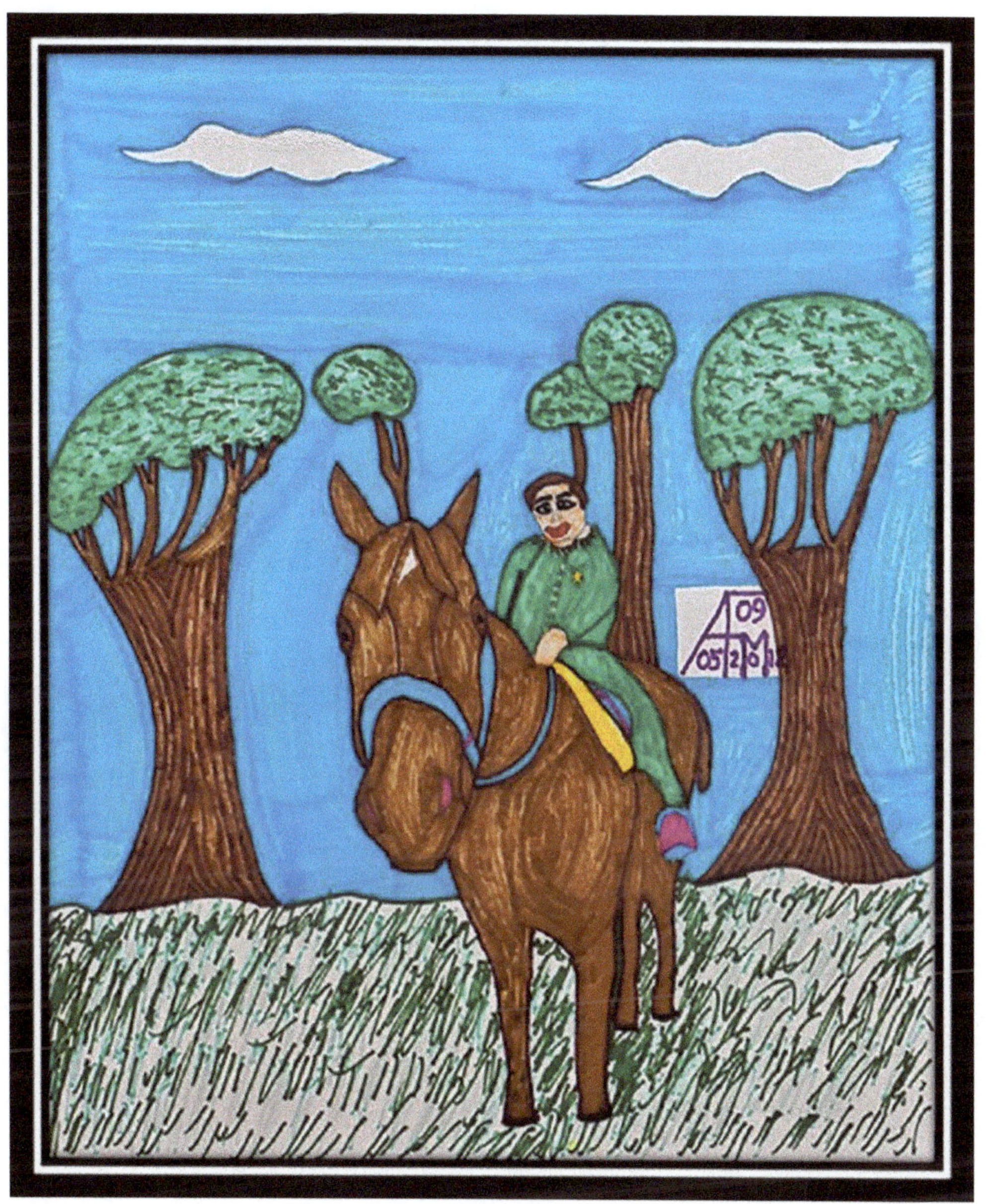

He Travels South

Gray Memory

Grandma's wrinkled skin of parchment,
Quiet whistle of her breath, her frail hand
Quivers slightly on her bed.
Age quickly approaches with much stealth.
Death is right outside her door.
Gone are the remembered times of joy.

Laughter at the table, cloudy swirls above
Mountains of sliced beef, orange carrots,
Pools of rich gravy that run down
Snow-white hills of creamy lumpy potatoes.
Silver slides across floral porcelain as the
Family catches each one's news.

Under the covers, her one leg now only a specter.
Pain wails down the long homebound hallway.
Death's poisons-stricken leg remaining.
Holidays warm and bright, home-made gifts
And treats from Mama's smiling parents
Open the flower of my love.

Love and sorrow enter, family visits
To say its last and silent goodbyes.
Another world spreads before her.
Her soft blue eyes see heaven alone.
Grandpa sits in prayer, his
Heart beats with hers.

I do not see him go the following
Year to quickly rejoin her.
The house is graying now, Dark rooms and empty.
Ghostly peace, laughter's echo rules.
Memories whisper, ease our pain of loss.

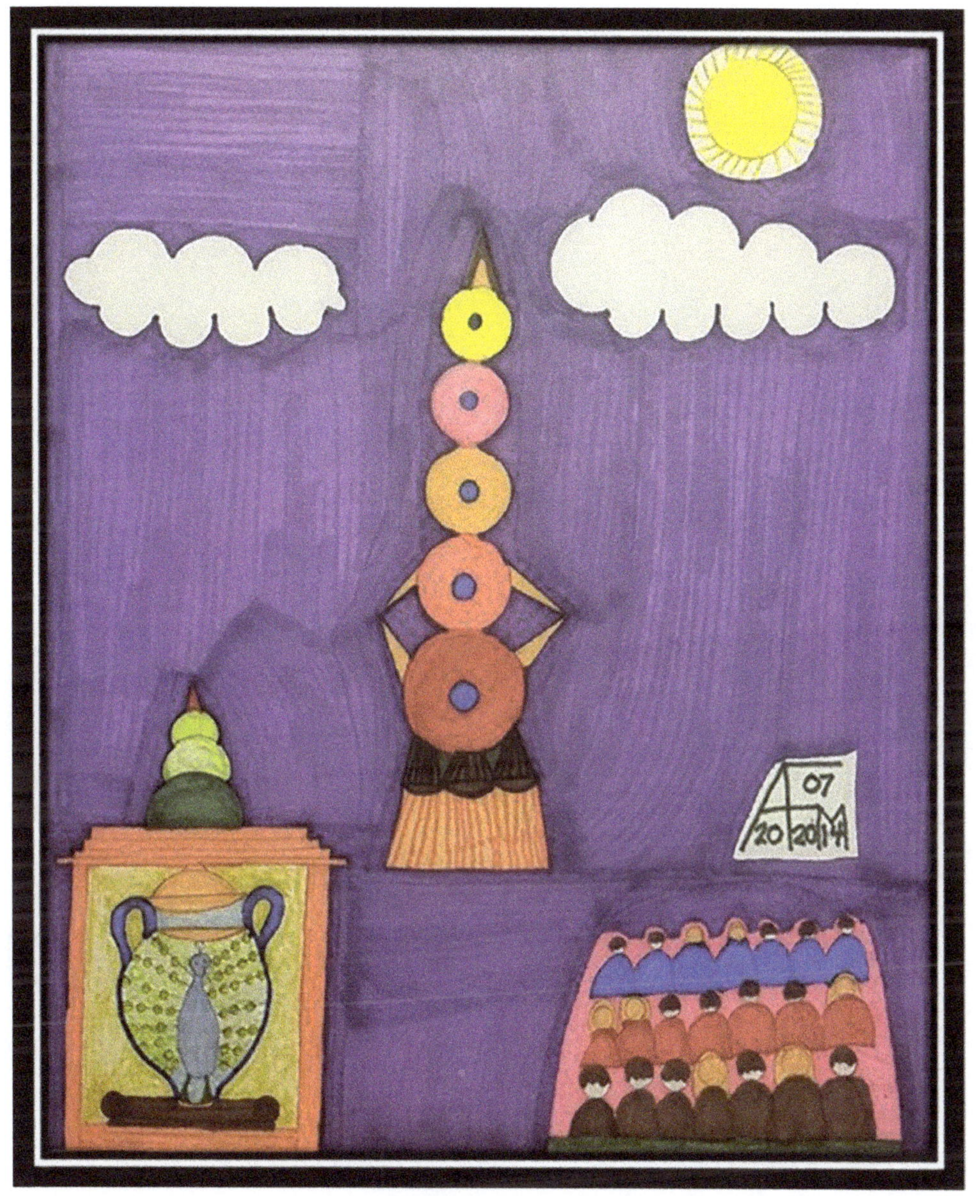

Mighty Ship from Andran Sky

Dream of Family Gathering

He comes to my dream
Of family gathering,
Welcome by all who
Remember him fondly.

Everyone acts as if he
Has just come back home
From an unknown journey,
Smiling at his return.

He doesn't even fool me.
I storm from dinner's table
At his tasteless deceit.
Dare he come after me?

A scrape of chair, his
Excuse to leave the room.
In entrance hall we talk.
Hatred on my face, tears.

I confront him, knowing he is dead.
No one will admit the awful truth.
I do not understand their denial.
What does he want of me?

Something I desire of him?
He cannot take back his
Lifetime of alcoholism.
Can I love him—faults and nobility?

Yet I'm unsure what part of
Him still lives within myself.
In my dreams and in my life,

I wish to discover this.
He's my dad, and I miss him
As much as the rest of my family.
I wish to hold him outside my dream.

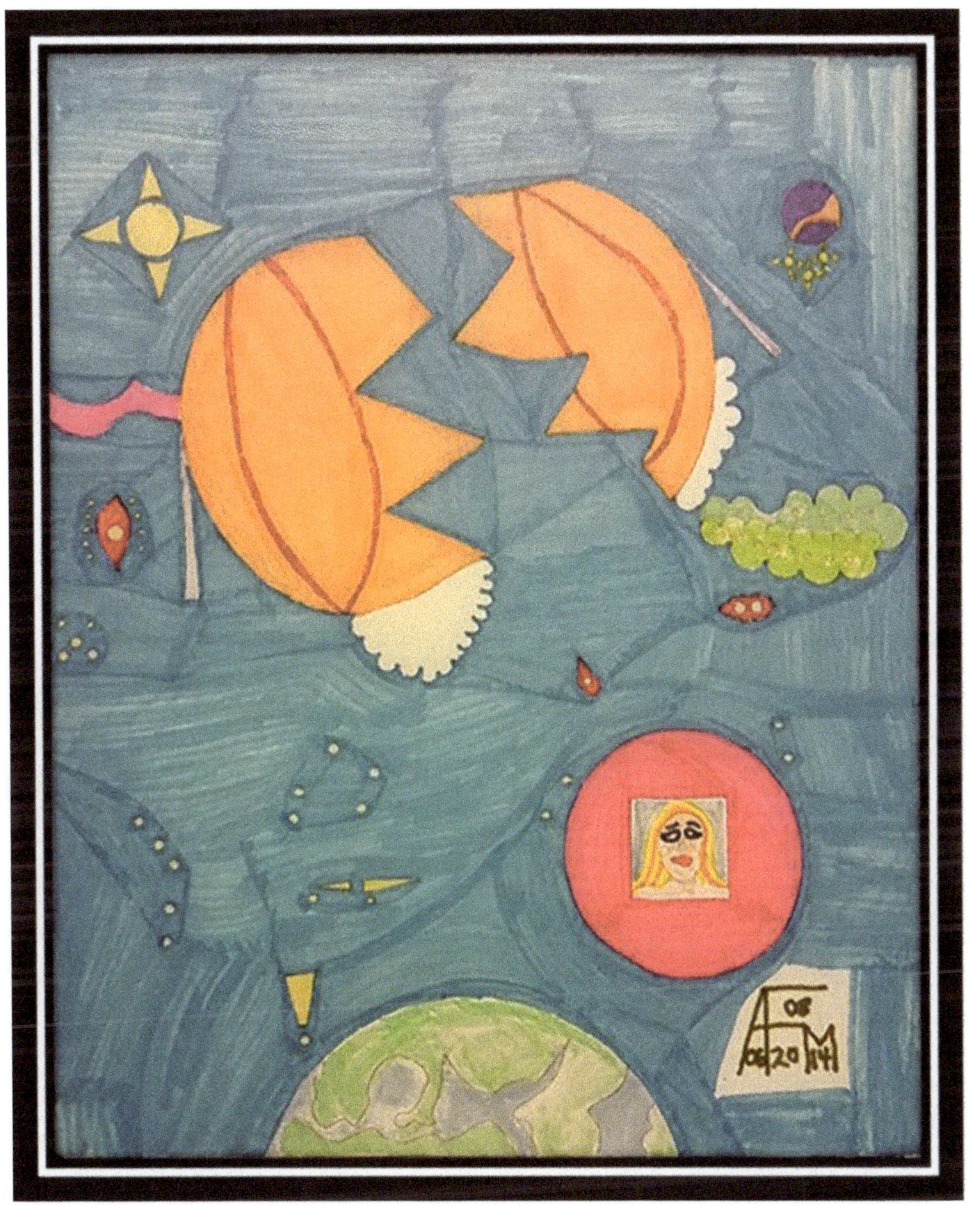

Systems Now Torn Asunder

Poverty Swallows Me Whole

I walk through gray slush,
Splatters beneath my feet.
Feels the way mushy apples do
Squeezed within your rough hand.

I leave my darkened room
With its eternal cold and
Lost cries of unfed kitties
Who want me back inside.

My key is broken in the chilled lock.
My life starts to break apart,
Seeming just as fore-shortened as
The useless brass stub in hand.

On what door might I knock?
Mother's door is closed today.
While poverty swallows me whole,
She's helpless to give me happiness.

Too late—a shelter closes in the
Face of my horror for the cold.
Too soon—another shelter requires
Intake interview for referral.

Cold, empty streets blur and fade
Beneath feet weary with tramping,
A call to city hotline for warm
Mattress finally finds me a place.

The sleepy outsider arrives
Searching for the unlocked door.
My last steps reach down to
Arms of sleep and brief comfort.

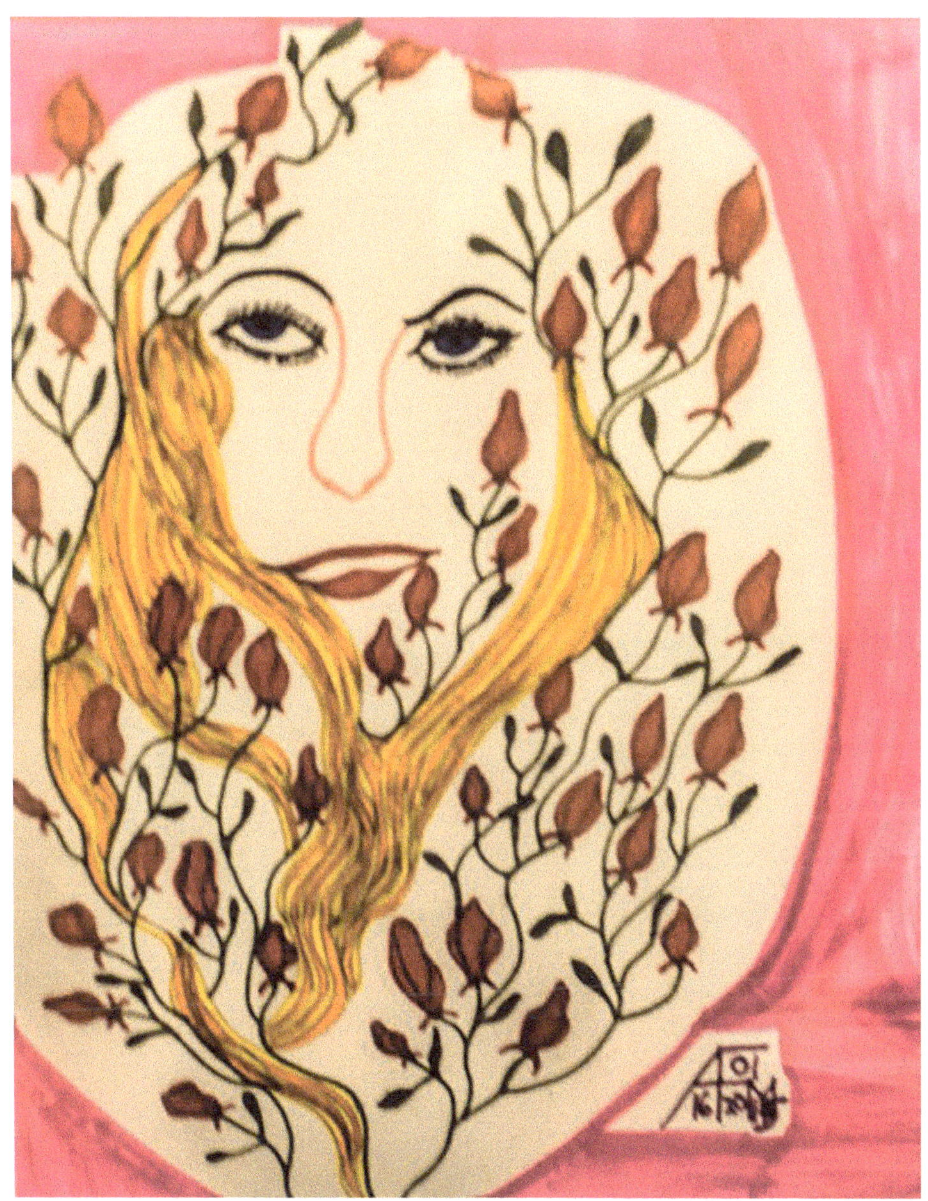

Heavenly Rose

Burned into Memories

For Nickie--

Her picture had just those
Colors of that sunset, subtle,
Dark and varied as her
Moods of quiet thoughts afire.

Burned into memories of
Freedom and clean air taken
Into her very spirit that
Soared above sharp peaks.

Brush into wet earth
Tones in oil, flies over
Canvas slate of new
Insight. Her audience

Only a silent orange
Feline. Eyes of mystery
Follow each stroke
Deliberate or accident.

Her room's four walls
Melt, its warmth cannot
Block the whisper of that
Snow-melt within her heart.

1/31/93

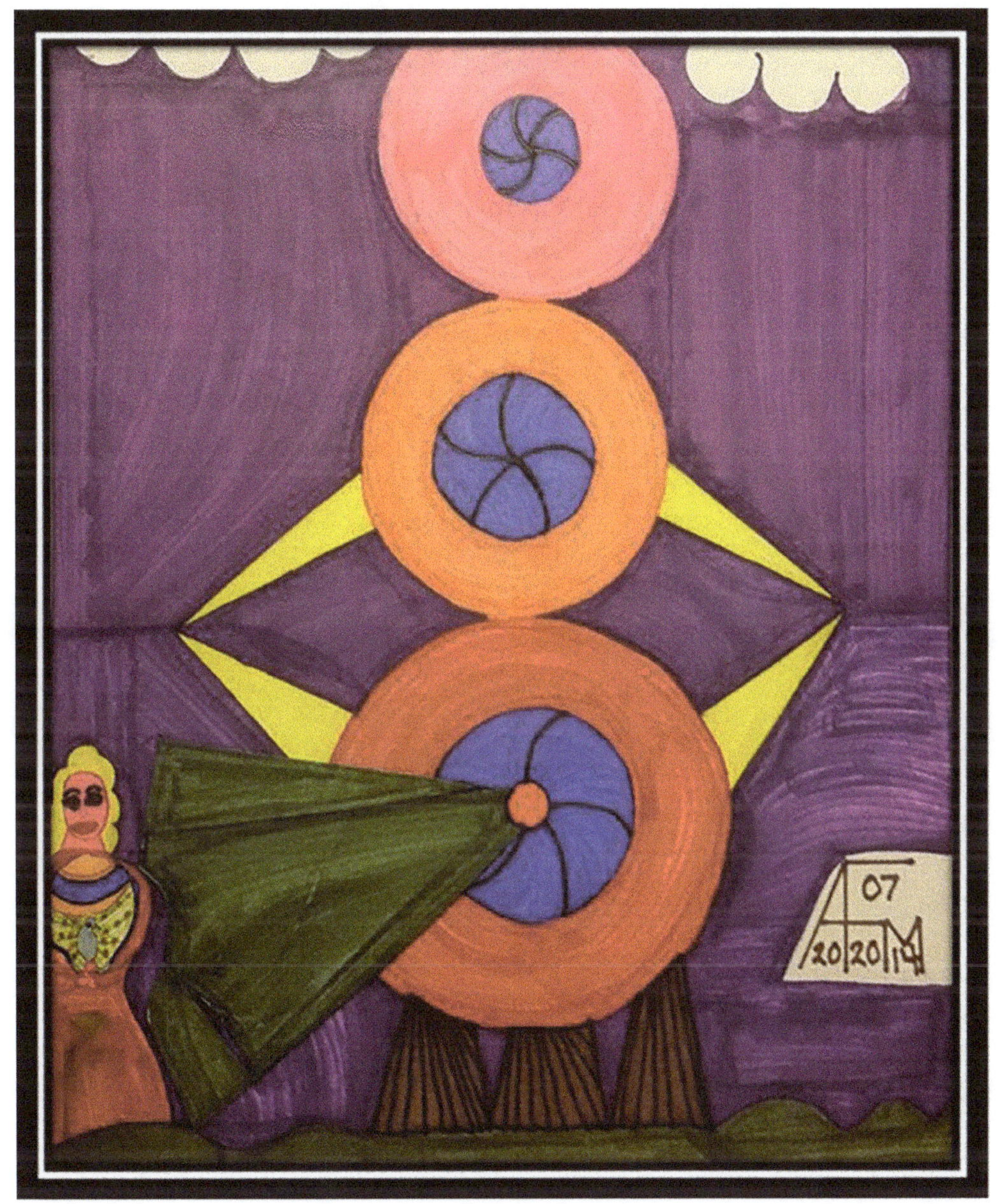

To Receive the Urn

Moon Is Love

Allen F. McNair©

November 6, 2017

As the moon appears from under a cloud
Our evening orb then shines so proud.
Thus, loving you, I soon nibble your ear
On a black night that arrives truly clear.

As under the moon we remain to meet.
Your lips are cherries so ripe and sweet.
They cling to mine so cool and wet.
You are, my love so dear my pet.

The stars soon come out to play.
The nightly ball is here to stay.
I bless the night more than the day.
My heart is a sponge, not made of clay.

My love for you is always and ever true.
I am ready to give all of my life to you.
Your skin, quite white against the moonlight,
Glistens bright with love's rich dew tonight.

You are so radiant with your passion.
My love for you is this night's fashion.
I long for your tender, warm embrace.
The moon's rays alight your open face.

Kiss me as many are the stars that loom.
You make me swoon before the moon.
And I can't believe that it's already June.
Four months we've loved under the moon.

The nightly part of the day is now ours.
Under the moonlight and the stars.
We own the night and all its parts.
We know the love that is in our hearts.

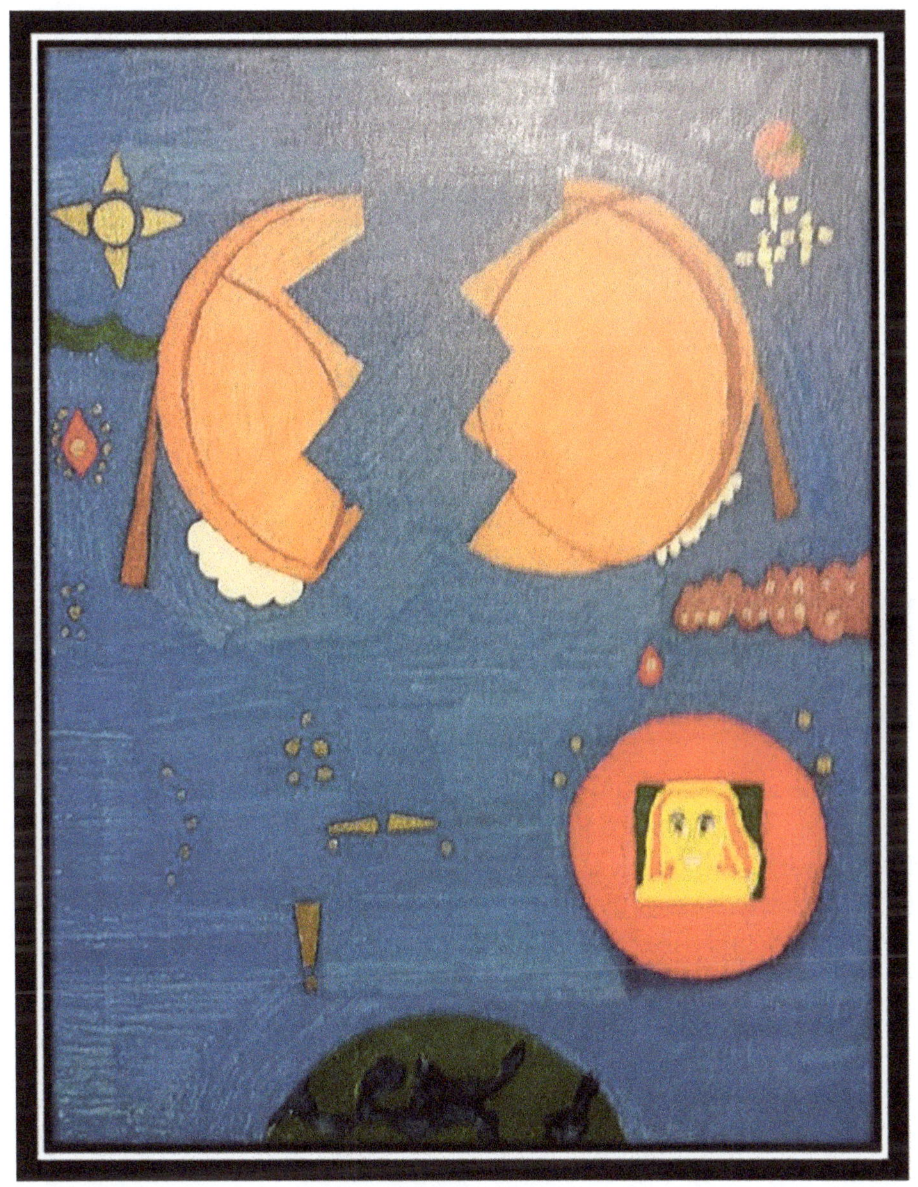

Adrift in Space

In the Realm of My Beloved

Allen F. M[c]Nair©   July 15, 2013

In the realm of my Beloved
I live beyond all care or pain.
I see my life anew from on high.
His arms enfold all that I am.

We are now one in mind and spirit.
Our world is an unbounded whole.
The material world is presently distant.
I find myself apart from it yet within.

I have all that I need within me.
My possessions no longer possess me.
My love can be shared with all.
I see my Creator's Love in all creatures.

Through my own dark night of the soul, I
experience signs of my Beloved's peace. It
is a balm that calms my fear of death.
Peace overcomes the challenge of change.

Before I lie down for my needed rest
I seek through closed eyes that dark night.
All of life's activities do cease.
Images come from within my consciousness.

Bubbles of light and bliss
Come from deep within.
They tickle me to sweet laughter.
I feel the warmth of His Love.

As I lie down, ready for sleep,
I feel encircled by a world of nurture.
My mother is at home in my heart.
She is alive, not actually dead to me.

Those loved ones since passed
Now surround me with their love.
Their smiles shed new light on me.
I am bathed awash in this light.

I bring this light to my world without.
Every last thing shines in brilliance.
Joy fills me up with all Love.
It makes everything in life sweet.

In God's Own Hands

In God's own hands, in God's own hands
For us all are His grand old heavenly plans.

Back in December 2013 my brother's
Father-in-law passed away at 96 years.
He was in failing health for the last few years.
His family felt their grief during Christmas.

In God's own hands, in God's own hands
For us all are His grand old heavenly plans.

More is the pity that I hardly knew him.
Yet the few vague memories that I have
Are of a vital man and his wife of many
Years in my own past life of vivacity.

In God's own hands, in God's own hands
For us all are His grand old heavenly plans.

His passing makes me think of everyone
In my life who are now gone from me.
I remember when I was twenty-three
My fifty-five-year-old father died.

In God's own hands, in God's own hands
For us all are His grand old heavenly plans.

My grief from his passing was mixed.
As Wilbur's eldest son from my mother,
I loved the man and hated his weakness
For drinks of the spirit in his brief life.

When I was fifty-one I lost my dear
Seventy-eight-year mother, Sylvia.
Although I was emotionally closer to her,
I always felt some distance from her love.

In God's own hands, in God's own hands
For us all are His grand old heavenly plans.

In 2010, my dear brother Roger
Died at fifty-four years of age.
I felt closest to him in personality.
We both felt the allure of electronics.

In God's own hands, in God's own hands
For us all are His grand old heavenly plans.

He would take me often to my destination
In his wonderfully grand old taxicab.
Only occasionally did I have to pay.
We shared the Harry Potter experience.

In God's own hands, in God's own hands
For us all are His grand old heavenly plans.

The heaviest toll taken in my life
Came when my closest companion
The beautiful old black-and-white
Twenty-year-old cat, Kit Kat died.

Hands (continued)

In God's own hands, in God's own hands
For us all are His grand old heavenly plans.

He went from me after thirteen years
Of joy and consternation for me.
As with everyone's life, his was full.
I have no regrets for his being with me.

In God's own hands, in God's own hands
For us all are His grand old heavenly plans.

With these deaths, I am aware
Of my own vulnerable mortality.
My sister, Patty, speaks of her own
Infirmities as we pass my father's age.

In God's own hands, in God's own hands
For us all are His grand old heavenly plans.

My brother Don will always be
The younger man in my life.
Who of us will leave this life first?
He seems to me the healthier.

In God's own hands, in God's own hands
For us all are His grand old heavenly plans.

The years of my wonderful life pass me by.
As I reach for the magic age of seventy-eight
I am aware of the potential for an end
Or a beginning to come upon me.

In God's own hands, in God's own hands
For us all are His grand old heavenly plans.

I will cherish every day as my last.
I will make the most of each day.
I will cherish the brief time that
We all have with each other.

In God's own hands, in God's own hands
For us all are His grand old heavenly plans.

Of This, I Relate and I Can't Wait

Allen F. M[c]Nair©

November 24, 2017

To tell of this experience, I cannot wait.
To all my friends I wish to relate
It just happened when I meditate.
Afterwards, I truly feel great.

Meditation helps to settle the mind.
No better means will you ever find.
It is taught by teachers who are certified
By the Teacher's Training Course, so fine.

Enjoyed this practice some forty years
Among a generation of my peers.
For this I am grateful to give many cheers.
This experience of bliss drives out all my fears.

I was peacefully in my meditative thrall.
I felt light as a feather overall.
The next feeling can't be overstated.
For me this time, I felt ever so elated.

I had this shift of body and of mind
As they both began to unwind.
For this experience I remain innocent.
Though in spirit, I feel quite magnificent.

The next moment seemed so very abrupt.
Was I coming down from being up?
Firmly placed in my seat by an outside force.
I continued to meditate to stay the course.

I look forward to twice-daily meditations.
And other experiences of real integration.
Besides endless progress in human relations.
This is only one of many sensations.

And so, as they say, I will take it as it comes.
I can't wait to relate this to my chums.
For me, meditation is so much fun.
And with all of this said, my poem is done.

The Scarecrow

Allen F. McNair©

December 10, 2017

After the farmer's harvest ends,
The scarecrow stands alone.
Forgotten by the harvesters who
Enjoy their bounty of fruits and vegetables.

Bright yellow corn and shining squash,
Pumpkin meat easily savored and ingested.
Shiny red apples rich in sweet flavor.
The garden feast enjoyed by all.

The Scarecrow actually scared no crows.
One wonders why he is there at all.
An iconic symbol of the farmer's wealth.
The silent guardian of all that he surveys.

He will be in his field for years to come.
He has been there for years before.
Several will be his owners who will
Come and go ad infinitum.

Children will come and play, thinking
Him to be a man, a teacher or preacher.
He looks at them and the field itself, sightless.
His eyes are hidden by the straw itself.

He will be in this field as more fruits
And vegetables then grow there.
Strong and vital will be the men
And women of each good harvest.

American heartland has countless
Scarecrows for each gathering.
Tradition has no sense of practicality.
These strawmen represent the owners themselves.

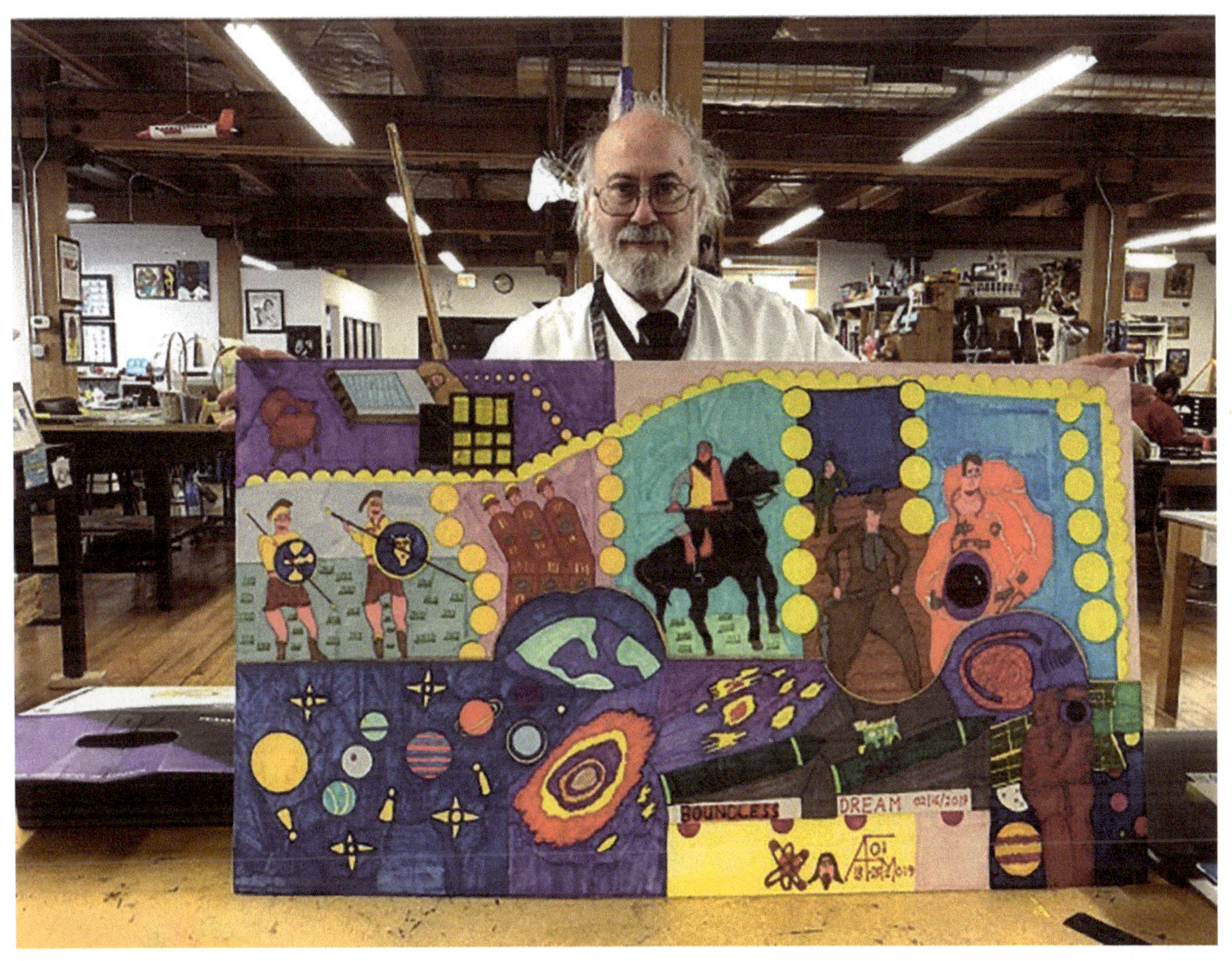

Boundless Dream
(2019-02-23)

Boundless Dream

Allen F. McNair©   April 18, 2012

Tonight, Ravel's *Bolero* takes me
To a vivid blessing of sleep.
As I lie in bed, images start to flash
Before me, columns of many nations.

First Greek soldiers march along
A wide, paved roadway, in black armor,
Their breastplates and shields gleaming.
Then a phalanx of Roman warriors comes.

Their armor a deep color of burgundy.
Behind them march medieval knights.
More strut on powerful horses proud.
Along the broad avenue doughboys walk.

The Hun also travels the roadway.
Next march friend and foe of World War II.
After them march men from the Korean
Police action and today's forces.

Finally, American astronauts and Soviet
Cosmonauts stride the wide highway.
Long rockets ride along the roadway.
They follow the travelers of the heavens.

All during the long march, the Ode plays
Ringing in my head, its rhythm strong.
My very limbs sing to the vibrant chorus.
I feel my head and heart soar to its beat.

Now my spirit is lifted on currents of
Wind and fire, up into the boundless sky.
I see nations and continents become small.
A blue and white globe comes into view.

Other worlds of a complete solar system
Appear before my celestial face and eyes.
A solar wind carries me ever outwards.
Soon other planetary systems are revealed.

Dream (continued)

Gradually I see a galaxy of stars and worlds.
My spirit itself expands to embrace them all.
My very body tingles with vibrations.
My mind beholds a truly grand, boundless dream.

I feel as one with humanity and the heavens.
All of the night and day are honestly me.
Understanding of the all-encompassing universe,
The tiniest atom of life's matter is also me.

But soon I awaken to my limited reality.
The bed sheets damp and twisted awry.
The two pillows under my head bunched-up.
The music is gone now, softly lost to my ears.

Tonight, I have only four walls to surround me.
The furniture hidden in the dark shadows.
My aching body once again a finite shell.
But I will always have my boundless dream.

Into all my tomorrows it enlivens a sense
Of joy for each day that I am alive.
An experience of conscious expansion of
My dreams for the future fills my soul.

This finite shell is not all that I am.
Joy and bliss are my birthright.
Unity with all that I perceive brings
Me closer to an awareness of God.

In the Realm of My Beloved--Revised

Allen F. McNair©   August 15, 2013

In the realm of my Beloved,
Beyond all care or pain
Life anew from on high.
His arms enfold all that I am.

Now one in mind and spirit,
Our world an unbounded whole.
The material is presently distant.
Myself apart from it yet within.

What I need is within me.
Objects no longer possess.
Love can be shared with all.
In every creature, my Creator's Love.

Through the dark night of the soul,
Signs of my Beloved's peace.
A balm that calms a fear of death.
Peace conquers the challenge of change.

Before my needed rest
Eyes closed seek that dark night.
Life's activities do cease.
Images come to consciousness.

Bubbles of light and bliss
Come from deep within.
They tickle me to sweet laughter.
I feel the warmth of His Love.

As I lie down, ready for sleep,
Encircled by a world of nurture.
Mother is at home in my heart.
Alive, not actually dead to me.

Those loved ones since passed
Now surround with their love.
Smiles shed new light on me.
I am bathed awash in this light.

Light comes to the world
Everything shines in brilliance.
Joy fills me up with all Love.
Life becomes sweet.

Butterscotch—Contented Cat

Allen F. McNair©   August 19, 2013

Butterscotch is a contented cat.
She likes to keep up conversation.
Her "meow" keeps me company.
Ever playful, she rubs me the right way.

Her white fur is tinged with orange.
Always talkative, she greets me
When I have come home to rest.
Her call to me always soothes.

Love swells my tender breast
Whenever she is near at hand.
I love to pet her lovely body.
She purrs then with satisfaction.

When I come through the door
From my travels, she stretches out,
Exposing her underbelly to my hand.
A seductress, she invites a petting.

As I first arrive from my travels,
She sniffs at me to assure herself
Of whom she greets at the door.
Satisfied, she marches forth and settles in.

She calls for her food in the early morning,
Watching me as she proceeds to her dish.
She wants me to follow and to witness
The empty dish, wanting to be fed soon.

When I am feeling restless, she reflects this.
She interrupts me with her soft caress
Of her languorous feline body against me.
She gently licks my hand, arms and chest.

These gentle kisses are insistent, determined.
They ardently speak consistently of her love.
I am kept awake to her constant need of me.
They speak of her sweet need of attention.

I am constantly reminded of there being
A creature in need of my consideration.
I cannot ignore her attention for very long.
No other business of mine is so important.

I feel there to be no loneliness
With her ever near to my side.
My need of loving is satisfied.
My constant companion is here.

God gave me a loving companion
To banish my various cares and woes.
My heart melts before her tender
Embrace, any harshness overcome.

Butterscotch is a contented cat.
She likes to keep up conversation.
Her "meow" keeps me company.
Ever playful, she rubs me the right way.

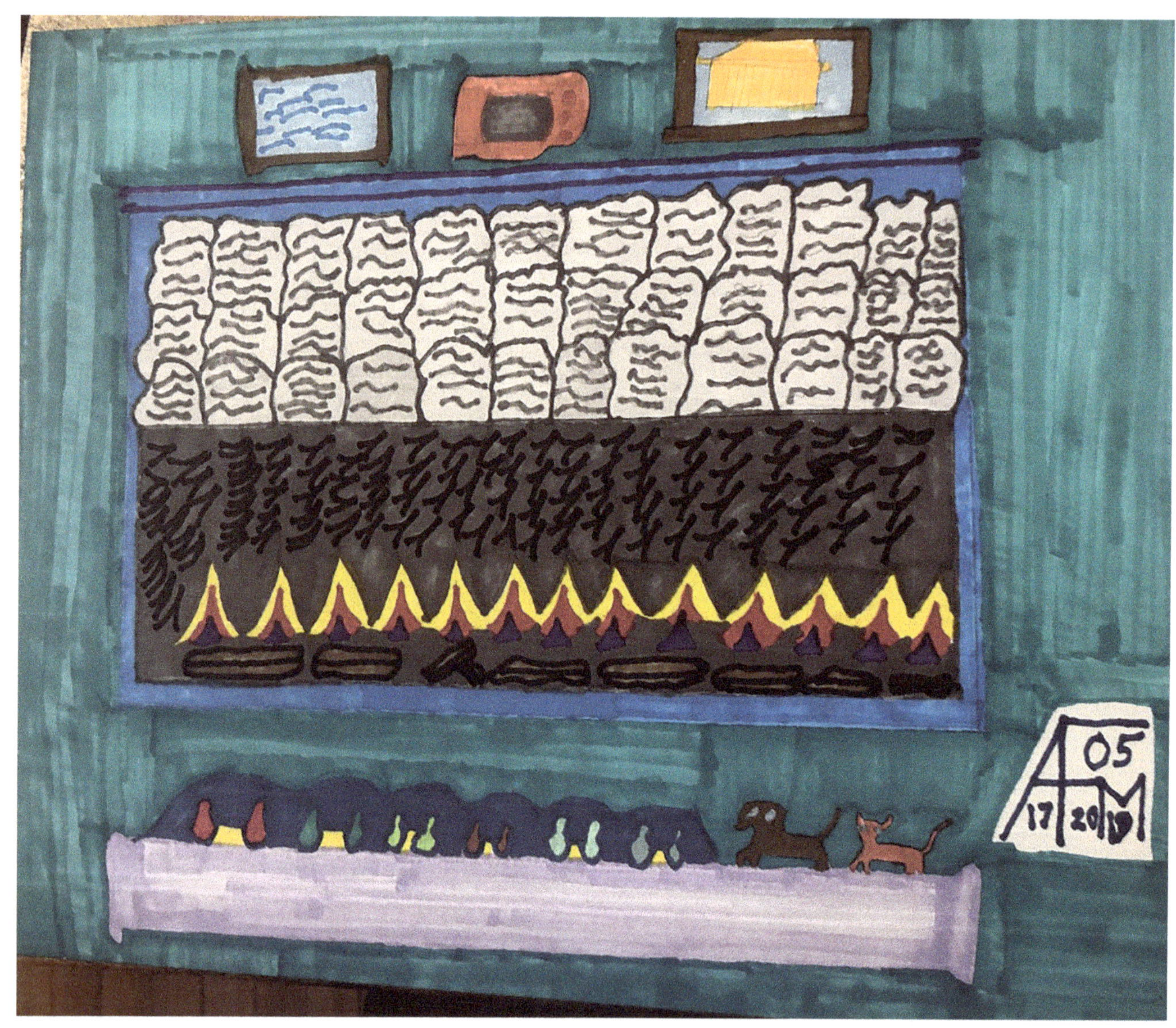

By the Roaring Fire
(2019-05-16)

By the Roaring Fire

I remember those always-cold winter nights
By the big, roaring fire in our stone fireplace.
Even the sprinkling of heaven's stars was cold.
We had only ourselves for warmth besides that fire.

A family of six—two parents, four young kids,
We would bundle up under several large blankets
Of a huge, king-sized mattress on the frosty floor,
Against the dead-cold of a dying central furnace.

Our strong father was a big bear of a man,
Our mother was a pretty as a picture painting.
We three sons bore his handsome facial features.
Our little sister was as good-looking as our Mom.

It was maple sugar time in Mom's old-time Vermont
Which we always celebrated at home in Chicago.
We had collected purely-driven powdered snow for
Our special New England brown maple syrup.

The taste of that melting snow on wooden plates
Was as sweet as love shining from our parents.
It just didn't matter if our family couldn't afford
To pay the heating bill for our central heater.

That day was warm enough in love for summer,
Bodies huddled and cuddled together against
The lasting cold of winter's abiding day.
But with each other close, we all felt it not.

Our family spent more than one winter thus.
But time passes us all and we grow older.
The bodies of others come to keep us warm.
And we are no longer close to each other today.

That big stone fireplace is long gone now, the
One-family house replaced by new four-flat.
No longer do we face the winter cold together.
Revised 06-07-2005

He's Long Gone Now

He's long gone now, along with the pain,
His heart gave out in a grocery store.
He was buying some cheese for a party.
Even his worn-out kidneys couldn't save him.

It was after a long battle with the bottle and
Keeping business and family responsibilities.
His unbounded spirit left his run-down body.
It winged its way to realms unknown.

He left behind five sons and a pretty girl-child.
His second son of the original six passed on before.
His farmland father proved himself the stronger.
He survived two of his three seeming hard stock.

My grandfather was always asking, asking
About my Dad's habits, did he drink or
Whether he smoked, asking, always asking.
What was I to say to the confrontations?

I lied in half-truths, saying he once did both
But has since quit for quite some time now.
Times uncounted, the same half-truths given.
Feeling the fool, trying to keep the peace.

But it happened one day, grandfather found
A wine rack outside my door with bottles full.
It didn't matter that my parents slept there
While he took the marital bedroom for himself.

My Dad spoke his own half-truth about it, the
Wooden wine rack was after all mine, he said.
Untold was that the bottles were his, after all.
I was condemned to be thought a slave to drink.

What doesn't kill us makes us stronger, they say.
And I have battled the wish of death many times.
But he is long gone now, along with the pain.
His unbound spirit winged its way to realms unknown.

When he passed on, I felt nothing for him.
But with each year's growth I feel that
He is very much a part of me and, so I
Believe, much of me belongs to him today.

Revised 06-07-2005

Communication of the Self

Allen F. McNair©   January 20, 2016
Revised March 11, 2017

There is a place where I like to go
Deep within my mind and heart.
It is a place of unbounded bliss
Which I enjoy relating to others.

An unlimited reservoir of creativity.
It allows me great wisdom to express
To others about life's experiences.
I am able to tap into it twice-daily.

It is an ocean of bubbling bliss which
Rises in waves of interminable joy.
Thoughts surge within consciousness
As I continue to dive within deeply.

Ideas effortless bubble up within as
Effervescent gems of quiet inspiration.
As a spiritual miner, I find real value in
These precious jewels of revealed truth.

I gently seek a deeper understanding
While my writing and illustrations grow
Inside my head, capable of natural fruition.
I am soon in the zone of great productivity.

When I go beyond my thoughts and feelings
I experience something much greater than
The finite mental sum of my actual parts.
It is a limitless field of all possibilities.

The deep-rooted stresses just melt away.
My mind is then freer than the wind.
This wind blows away the clouds of
Ignorance and my distorted thinking.

Many of the poems I write provide New
insights into others' character. They
illuminate the lessons of my life as
The rays of the midday sun clear the sky.

The feelings and thoughts of each poem
Reach universal truths in my constant
Effortless communication of the Self.
Without poetry, I could not communicate.

Just a few words of title or theme rapidly
Expand to complete stories in poetry.
I am able to paint solid word-pictures 7
That have been transformed to artworks.

The Self (continued)

These works of art illustrate my poetry
As a spotlight eliminates a darkened room.
The shadows of mystery soon disappear
From abstract concepts transcribed in pen.

The energy expended in telling these stories
Is really quite minimal to my versatile mind.
An inner intelligence directs the flow of
Narrative as my poems unfolds directly.

Going to my place of rest and tranquility
Transforms the individual self to cosmic Self.
From the small world, nuggets of wisdom arise
Into a grand universe of unbounded perspective.

The Self is all there is within each person.
Anyone has access to this infinite Self.
I have had this experience for over forty years
Since instructed in Transcendental Meditation.

This easy and effortless technique of mental
Exploration expands the mind immeasurably.
New ideas manifest themselves with fascinating
Food for one's intellectual appetite to be satiated.

Poetry is the universal expression of one's thoughts.
Its great importance is very real, especially to me.
Individual pieces about homelessness and its adventures
Have progressed into an epic poem set in the future.

My mind and heart have also grown apace.
Poetry has given me a voice to be heard.
My own world is a better place originating
From thoughts and progressing into words.

These tremendous thoughts are vessels upon
A sea of tranquility and peace within my mind.
They float without effort to be discovered anon.
I gather them together to ship cargos of sagacity.

As I transcribe my thoughts to paper for readers,
Words miraculously appear to express concepts
Grand and wondrous and I progress in poetry.
From single stories, I develop grander visions.

My wish to be self-published has borne fruit
My epic poem, *I Dream of A'maresh,* has
Taken root in the minds of many readers
Both in the recent past and soon into the future.

A fortress for commanding a vast territory of
The field of literature awaits my use of pen in
Magical arenas of storytelling upon the stage
Of tremendous auditoriums in my future spent.

I look forward to telling other stories every day.
With the constant communication of the Self
There is no end to what I can express to all.
And poetry actually makes all of this come true.

The Growth of Hope

Allen F. McNair©   January 20, 2016

The growth of hope dawned on me one
Dreary night as I lay in my bed after
Weeks of homelessness, when I realized
I was on the thresholds of new housing.

I was soon to be transferred from a shelter
To a newly-created group home on Keystone.
It was proposed to me over a welcome lunch with the
Kind administrators from Lutheran Social Services.

I could not have conceived of such good fortune
Several months living in the Lakeview shelter.
Yet I was given a gentle challenge to stay in
The shelter only if I worked to grow out of it.

I had worked with the city's social service network
To establish my actual mental disability status.
I had a kindly psychiatrist who understood my true
Nature of mental health with diagnosis of bipolar disorder.

I was now taking the right medication and adjusted well.
Since I had a history of stable employment before
Homelessness found me emotionally stricken and unwell,
I would be working and receiving the benefits of Disability.

Growth (continued)

As I grew emotionally, I began to write stirring poetry
For a social services' literary magazine, the *Musing Place.*
I began to perform my poetry onstage in the Thresholds
Program of Theater Arts at the Blue Rider theater.

I also worked in theater maintenance through this program.
It was a new, productive means of expression for me.
Even before this, I performed my poetry in the ensemble
Work of a collaborative venture called *Address Unknown.*

I was being highly productive even while homeless
And now I would embark on the new journey of
Actual housing with employment and writing poetry
Has been my lifeline to the shore of home and work.

Poetry has also opened up the door of drawing, painting,
And other such creativity, including my own art exhibit.
The Literary Guild once owned a bookstore on Lincoln
In the jolly old town of rocking Chicago, Illinois.

In their store, I was once in a Thresholds-sponsored show.
Impressed with some of my work, I was given a show
Of my own which featured all the women I had never met.
Of the pieces sold, one was bought at its asking price.

Growth (continued)

Although originally bought for less, he paid the actual
Difference soon after he saw its true value to himself.
I truly saw the progress from writing poetry in words
To illustrating its content in grand expressions of art.

Poetry is my life's ambition as well as other forms of art.
Many times, when considering an end to my own life
Another poem comes to my fevered mind to complete,
Providing a constant source of miraculous hope for me.

Now I have regularly contributed to whole anthologies
In the now extinct form of *Journal of Ordinary Thought*.
I have also continued to perform my poetry in open
Readings at the Bazazian Public Library on Ainslie.

My life continues to grow in hope as I continue to write.
Poetry has rescued me from the very jaws of death.
I look ahead at the brightness of a future in writing.
I am ready to master life's challenges with a sense of hope.

Electronic Nirvana

Allen F. M[c]Nair©

August 18, 2013

Happy 62nd Birthday to me!
The day started with brunch
With my family, receiving cards
And gifts of money. Hooray!

Plans to spend the new resources
Fomented in a feverish brain.
I negotiated to spend less
With assorted coupons.

Now there is a keyboard for
My new tablet, easing writing
Messages to my many friends.
New storage space for files abounds.

Office 365 includes SkyDrive.
Documents from the computer
Are now downloaded without effort
Into a tablet-friendly office app.

A Galaxy Note tablet and a Galaxy
S4 phone are now my electronic
Generators of my creative texts.
I am now in electronic heaven!

Just close the saved file on
My computer and voila—the
File can be accessed on cell or tablet
As long as I remember the password.

What electronic Nirvana awaits me,
Making any environment a virtual
Home office for my creativity.
My special day immensely satisfies.

Life today is a happy holiday.
Its usual depression miles away.
I am ready to face whatever
Now comes my way, triumphant.

Glory of Creation

Allen F. McNair©   May 29, 2015

When we are established in God Consciousness
We directly experience the Glory of Creation.
It is an experience beyond the syllables and sounds
Of the relative noise of everyday life in wakefulness.

We are familiar with the three major states of consciousness:
The state of non-existence of ourselves in deep sleep;
The delightful illusory state of dreaming the impossible;
The pleasant yet sometime tumultuous waking state.

I have come to know intimately a fourth state of Being.
Wherein I have experienced my Self alone, unbounded.
There is no single object of perception in this state of
Unbounded perpetual charm, bliss and wakefulness.

This state, transcendental consciousness, is the birthright
Of me, you and everyone in God's own Creation.
It is my experience that is beyond time and space boundaries.
I discover the source of everything twice daily through diving.

I constantly let go of this world's heavy cares daily.
The calm expansiveness now pervades even my outer
Experience of the dynamism of the everyday activity.
The bliss of eternal union with the divine constantly grows.

Glory (continued)

I have often dreamed impossible fantastical worlds
With an awareness of being in my own bed asleep.
I have had glimpses of the witnessing state known
As Cosmic Consciousness in even my deepest sleep.

Yet the most glorious state beyond this fifth state
Has even captured my outer awareness twice now.
My experience delightfully came one pleasant evening
In the small town of Livingston Manor, New York.

I had just finished an average meditation of transcendence.
I was coming downstairs to the facility's dining room
For an evening meal of fresh steamed vegetables,
Delicious roasted chicken and fluffy mashed potatoes.

When I stepped into the room of nice aromas
I innocently became aware of a golden halo
That surrounded and pervaded my senses
Of every object and person, I perceived.

This experience of the glory of life caused
A deep sense of peace and utter contentment
Abiding within my conscious waking state
Bubbling bliss caused waves of silent laughter.

Glory (continued)

A perpetual smile crossed my bright face.
I was cast in a beautiful glow of wonder.
The five senses vibrant to my awareness.
This current description pales by comparison.

Language pales in its expression of this
Infinite state of God realization to this day.
The finest value of celestial vision lasted
Only for the space of an hour's time.

Everyday objects of my perception
Were precious to my truest Self.
I couldn't sustain this precious state.
Eventually it left my perceptions of reality.

The memory brings tears of glorious joy.
It is vivid to me in its fleeting nature.
Back in 1974, I soon left the establishment
For the humdrum of everyday routine.

This life-transforming set of circumstance
Was not to be known in a repeatable form.
Yet it was not one that was suggested to me
By any description I had previously encountered.

Years later in a beautiful video I learned
From Maharishi Mahesh Yogi, who
Rediscovered the innocent and systematic
Procedure of Transcendental Meditation,
The knowledge of appreciation intellectually.

Glory (continued)

If we can perceive the colorless sap
Throughout the levels of its reality
And on its surface simultaneously
We can know the flower's true glory.

Yet this experience came to me first before its brilliant description.
Having transcended even those peaceful, sleeping elephants of
Deep-rooted stresses, I had come to expressly know life's bliss.
At the finest level of the transcendent reality I felt connected.

But everyday life had all but intruded
To temporarily banish me from the
World of this certain reality for years
Of my interesting and curious life.

Then last February 2015, the ultimate source
Of delight and peace returned in my awareness.
I had just finished learning and practicing
My third advanced technique of meditation.

I sat in a beautiful lounge of someone's home
Where I was taught my special technique.
I was nursing a delicious cup of tea.
The golden halo soon permeated the room.

Glory (continued)

Waves of gentle laughter consumed me.
Every object was soon surrounded by this glow.
I saw a flickering sparkle of life's reality
In my vision on its periphery of vision.

Yet soon this vision's splendor of glory faded.
An eagerness to tell someone of my experience,
To quietly confirm its existence within me and to
Receive some validation of its true nature consumed me.

I related this experience to one of the teachers
Of the basic Transcendental Meditation technique.
He had received many years of knowledge from
The great sage Maharishi through the miracle of video.

Steeped in his own direct experience of
Life's transcendence and the copious
Body of intellectual understanding,
He delighted me with his confirmation.

Glory (continued)

Today I look forward to further experience
And confirmations of my life's journey.
I am certain of gaining wisdom and inner strength.
The road to eventual enlightenment excites me.

The ultimate unity of my Being along with
The bliss of eternal union, the synthesis
Of the opposites of inner silence and the outer
Dynamics of activity quietly attracts me entirely.

The intellect's confirmations of direct experience
Encourages me to innocently anticipate the future—
From full integration of Cosmic Intelligence to
Stepping onto the plain of God Consciousness.

I am as certain of an eventual experience of
Unity Consciousness to come, as surely as
The temporary glimpses of nature's true reality
Which I have been privileged to intimately know.

Let me gently release all of life's stress
In each period of meditation daily.
Let me absorb each new experience.
Let me receive life's precious bounties.

All glory to my God, all glory to Maharishi,
All glory to Guru Dev, and to the precious
Tradition of their Vedic Masters.
I surrender to the Will of God Eternal.

Enjoying the Pandora Sound

Allen F. McNair©   August 18, 2013

As I type my document
I enjoy the Pandora sound
Produced on my tablet.
Its wondrous melodies resound.

With each song I do relate.
Its message coincides with
My most intimate experience.
When I am blue, I hear the blues.

If I feel cheated of love,
I have a song of the cheatin' kind.
When I am immersed in a project
I cannot put aside, I hear "Wild Horses."

The internet radio goes along with me.
At home my computer sings fantastic.
Taking public transportation becomes
More bearable as I listen to this music.

I am not feeling so helpless in life
When I listen to the song "Help."
I feel connected to others as I see
People with headphones and cell phones.

I am now closer to each stranger
Listening as I do, electronically.
Their lives not so different than mine.
I enjoy the variety of devices that abounds.

When listening to the tablet's sound
I hear an alert to know that my phone
Just this minute is calling for my answer.
I cannot ever miss an urgent call.

My electronics coordinate a new life.
I feel up-to-date with technology.
I am ready to share this experience
With the uninitiated who desire it.

Music conquers fears of inadequacy.
It mirrors one's life experiences.
Men and women, young and old,
Are united as avid listeners together.

My Two Worlds--Revised

Allen F. McNair©

June 4, 2017

I once lived in two worlds altogether.
The First is one of accomplishment,
Of college degree and literary
Talent readily acknowledged.

This first world is filled with the
Promise of a brilliant future,
Easily earned and rewarding
In its great potential for growth.

The other is of abject poverty and
Cold, thoughtless residence, of
Shelter filled with unknown men
And careless, heartless agencies.

I am filled with high anxiety.
Uncertain about my prospects.
The next meal feels elusive.
Depression fills my soul.

In the past, I looked out of
A warm-lit clothing store
To see a ragged woman—she
Seemed as distant as the moon.

I was content to be myself as
I shopped for my wardrobe.
I held myself in high regard
For my ability to provide.

My first world is of brightly colored
Books and new clothes not yet worn.
It speaks of money and belonging.
But I retreat from it, apart from it.

And join the army of walking wounded,
The untapped potential of the real people
Who walk the bombed-out streets beside
The false display of life's riches.

Yet I am filled with serious hope
For reconstructing my previous life.
I have promises to keep for myself,
Ready for the miles toward recovery.

While I rebuild the first world,
My heart remains open to bring
Along the real people that I've met
Into my future dreams and yours.

Compassion Moves a World

Allen F. McNair©   June 30, 2017

When compassion moves a world,
People will come together soon.
Everyone will rally to each other
With a love that can stir their hearts.

When compassion moves a planet,
Nations will live in peace eternally.
And borders will become truly passé.
The walls between ourselves will crumble.

When compassion soon rules our hearts,
Women and men will live in true equality.
Children will recognize their brothers in
The nature of their hearts instead of colors.

When compassion opens, each other's being
Will radiate as the stars' full light beams.
Our world will fully illuminate everyone's auras
Of joy and camaraderie in full effulgence.

When compassion begins to light up our globe,
Wars will cease to command our ignorance.
Brothers and sisters will dance in joyful song.
Religions will find their common ground in beliefs.

When compassion rings true in every heart,
Sadness will be a feeling of our distant past.
The bells will ring together as one joyous chord
From every mountaintop through every valley low.

When compassion stirs every living soul,
The very fertile soil will ripen in fruitful harvest.
Rich fruit and grain will fill every contented person.
Deprivation will no longer ring on any open door.

Let compassion be found in a mother's arms,
Encircling her child in one fond embrace.
Let each one of us enfold the other in joy.
And join in one bright song of togetherness.

To Die in Her Arms

Allen F. McNair©

February 5, 2014

Why can't I have the love of a woman?
To be held in her loving embrace,
To have her mouth enclosed in mine,
Would be something surpassing sweet.

I would willingly die in her arms
To all that I have or want to have.
I would give her my last penny
And take the food from my lips.

My friends do encourage me to be alone
Rather than seek a woman who asks much.
To be needed as no other would be needed
Becomes the siren call to sacrifice all that I have.

Alone among friends, I am already as dead.
Oh, why can't I die in some beloved's arms?
Yet I would want something material
Instead of Love's own conditioning.

To Die (continued)

Are love's physical needs so much more
Than having finances correct and orderly?
Or is having something, perhaps a cell phone,
Mean that I have what I actually love?

I wrestle with thoughts of ownership,
Of desires for love supreme, both
Complicated by needs uncounted.
I must have them without consequence.

Give me someone's love divine.
Make the spirit and material one
In a grand union of one person
With the body of another.

That I may accept the other person's faults
Without feeding such imperfections to grow,
I must simply enjoy my love of her without
Loving whatever she does apart from me.

To Die (continued)

Her desires are mostly material,
She wishes for financial means
To give her the support she craves.
I identify with these cravings.

My wish merely to help her as any soul mate
With unsecured financial assistance proves
Worse than being outright alone if I otherwise
Refuse to provide this means of support.

Can I give up my attraction to be needed?
Can I hold my beloved accountable for her
Debts to me or shall I write them off the
Ledger of my personal need for someone?

Only giving this relationship its time
For growing or just stagnating
Seems possible for me today.
I cannot decide its fate permanently.

Oh, to die in her arms would be preferable
To the living Hell without her love for me.
My material being longs for her physically.
Why can't I have a love that is eternal?

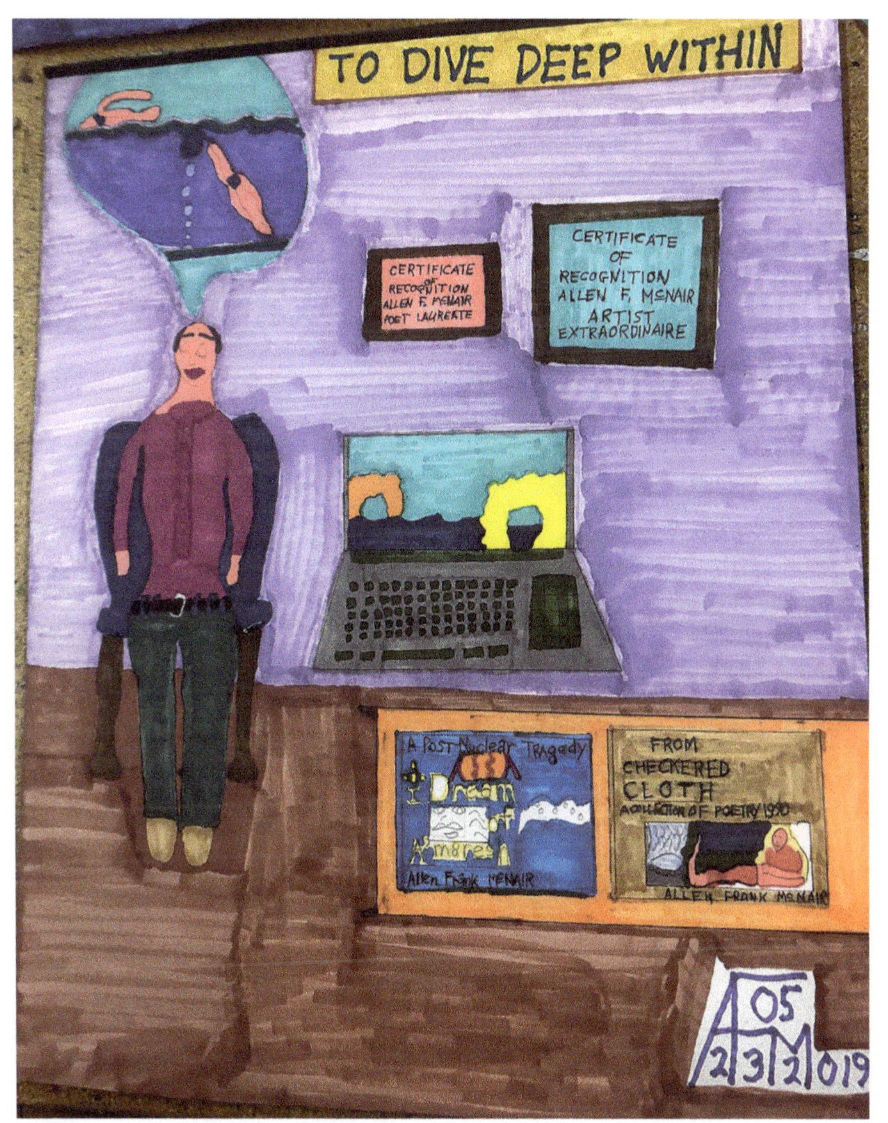

To Dive Deep Within
(2019-05-24)

To Dive Deep Within

Allen F. McNair©   August 25, 2013

To swim on the surface of the vast sea,
Skimming among its many waves.
Then prepare to dive deep within,
I let go of cares to trust in God.

Let go, the dive is sweet perfection,
Ever deeper to an area of calm.
Large bubbles of thought come.
Then, ever smaller bubbles beneath.

Descend ever deeper, the ocean's motion
Subsides, the deeper levels surge less.
The peace of the waters mirrors the calm.
The outside noise more distant.

Every motion also comes to rest
Without any thoughts distress.
An inner silence surrounds.
This silence within swells.

Now rise to the ocean's surface.
Carry forth silence into activity.
Swimming back to the distant shore,
The journey home is swift and sure.

The expansion of calmness carries me
Forward to my home of the senses.
In this expanded consciousness
They do not rule over me.

Optimism abounds in great energy.
Bright thoughts carry over into actions.
Creativity grows into great productivity.
Grand artwork, terrific poetry come forth.

Problems large become small.
Solutions elusive come readily.
At once renewed, the end is in sight.
Attainable goals, now certain.

The waters of life surround, uplift.
An abiding peace comes within,
Giving strength to live again.
I am now humbly invincible.

About the Author

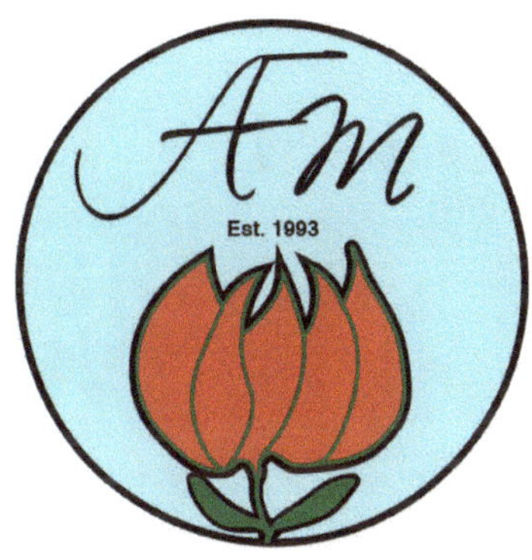

Allen F. McNair©   1997

I, Allen F. McNair am a member of Thresholds, which is a psychosocial rehabilitation organization, as well as a self-taught artist and poet who is inspired daily by the wonders of life around me, my present and past experiences, and both the inner and outer beauty of all women.

I have a Bachelor of Arts degree from Columbia College here in Chicago. I am a recent graduate of Wright College's Information Processing Technology class, where I studied the application of Microsoft Word, Excel, Access, and PowerPoint programs.

I recently produced an anthology of poetry entitled *From Checkered Cloth* which highlights some of my best work to date. I can be heard at Open Mike nights around the city, sharing my poetry.

I have performed in an original production based on true stories for the Thresholds Theater Arts Project at the Theater Building. Prior to the thespian work done through Thresholds, I had joined the ensemble cast of previously homeless performers in the play, "Address Unknown". In this play, we tackled the various aspects of the contemporary stigma of the homeless condition. I have also taught classes in creative writing and performance at both the National Alliance for Mentally Ill (NAMI) and at Trilogy.

I love watching science fiction, fantasy, and action in movies and reading those genres in literature in my spare time. I live in a studio apartment in Chicago with my 12-year-old long-haired black and white cat, Kit Kat.

About the Author—Allen F. McNair

Allen F. McNair©

November 1, 2017

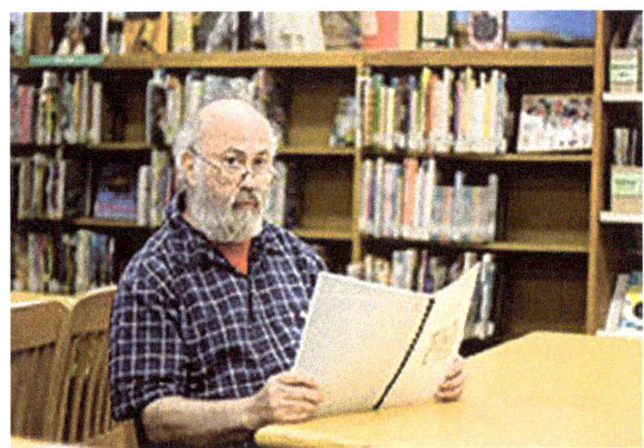

I am an author and self-taught artist who is inspired daily by the wonders of life around me, my present and past experiences, and both the inner and outer beauty of all women. From individual poetic portrayals in my early years of writing, I have graduated to writing an epic saga mentioned below.

I have enjoyed writing since I was six years old, adapting themes from Western dramas and comic books for my own entertainment and for imagined audiences world-wide. In 1990, I seriously began composing short poetry and published these works in Thresholds *Musing Place* magazine, a publication to which I was a contributing editor. Much of my poetry was primarily based on my temporary experience with homelessness.

My proudest achievement is the self-publishing of my book, *I Dream of A'maresh*, a science fiction epic poem of romance which I wrote and illustrated. I have shown a few of these illustrations in public showings. Some of its artwork were seen in the 27th American Disabilities Act Celebration at the James R. Thompson Center July 17 through July 22, 2017. A few of these works of art were once displayed in the July 2015 ADA Celebration at the same location. Some of them were shown at the Orange Restaurant in Lincoln Park last April 4, 2016. Others were also presented at the Orange Restaurant in Roscoe Village March 10 through May 28, 2015. I have likewise exhibited my artwork at the Gallery Cabaret in August 2106 and again in that same month of 2017.

I have performed in an original production based on true stories for the Thresholds Theater Arts Project at the Theater Building. I have also taught classes in creative writing and performance at both the National Alliance for Mentally Ill (NAMI) and at Trilogy.

In September of 2011, I was very happy to have secured a job at Mariano's Fresh Market on my own initiative and continued to work for the company until I retired October of this year. I am looking forward to further distinguishing myself in the writing and illustrating areas of my life in the years ahead.

I love watching science fiction, fantasy, and action in movies and reading those genres in literature in my spare time. I once lived in a one-bedroom apartment in Chicago with my 7-year-old white and ginger cat, Butterscotch until I gave her up to the Treehouse Animal Shelter due to reasons of her poor health. Previously, I had a black and white long-haired cat named Kit Kat, who lived to be 20 years old.